History Of The Beswick Cooperative Society Ltd.: From 1892-1907

A. E. Worswick

HISTORY

.. OF THE ..

BESWICK
Co-operative Society Ltd.

From 1892 to 1907.

—

... COMPILED BY ...

A. E. WORSWICK, F.C.I.S.,

Secretary to the Society.

MANCHESTER:
Co-operative Wholesale Society's Printing Works, Longsight.

—

1907.

Introduction.

———

CONSIDERING that it will be somewhat of interest to the members to possess a History of their Society, we have decided to publish an account of the Soc ety's establishment and progress, as far as can be gleaned from the records deposited in the archives.

We further hope that the publication may remove many misunderstandings which we know exist in the minds of some of our members as to the true origin of the Beswick Co-operative Society.

The compilation of this work does not celebrate any particular event, but to place the Society in its true position before the members. The period covered is only a matter of fifteen years, so that the reader must not anticipate details of such interest as might have been recorded had it been the Society's Jubilee.

The intention is to make the volume as readable as possible; and although histories, mostly interesting and instructive, are generally considered dry, we trust that by the finis is reached our endeavour to make it instructive of the Society's origin and of its phenomenal progress is attained, and that it may find a place in each member's bookcase.

THE COMMITTEE.

———

The photographs produced in these pages have, with one or two exceptions, been taken by the Society's photographer, Mr. E. J. Care, Beswick Studio, Ashton New Road.

CONTENTS.

ILLUSTRATIONS.

NEW CENTRAL PREMISES, ROWSLEY STREET, BESWICK.
(Opened August 13th, 1904)

CHAPTER I.

1892.—Formation.

A SHORT time prior to the opening of the year 1892 a feeling was expressed by several local gentlemen that the Co-operative movement was rather neglectful of Beswick and its immediate vicinity, and that its influence would be greatly felt by the poorer inhabitants if introduced.

With the object of providing this long-felt want in view a then influential local tradesman offered his grocery and provision business, situate at 30, Ashton New Road, Beswick —the very centre of the neglected district—to a neighbouring Society, whose nearest branches were about 1¼ miles apart.

They, however, refused to move in the matter; so, therefore, the body of gentlemen above referred to met in the office of Mr. A. Cuss to consider the situation. They decided to call a public meeting for the purpose of considering the desirability or otherwise of starting a new Co-operative Society to cater for the wants of Beswick and district—a district, large and congested, composed of working people.

The public meeting was held on January 22nd, 1892— slightly over fifteen years ago—in the Congregational Schools, top of Every Street. Mr. Arthur Cuss occupied the chair. The tradesman, Mr. John T. Dobson, enthusiastic in his endeavour to bring about Co-operation in his district, again offered his business as a nucleus for a progressive Society.

A passing reference might be made explaining the reason of his enthusiasm, which can readily be understood when mention is made of the fact that he had been an employé of a Co-operative Society before commencing business on his own account.

In offering his business to this meeting Mr. Dobson ably propounded the principles of Co-operation, and the benefits to be derived therefrom by the working classes. There is only one kind of Co-operation: the one with the same

principles as introduced by the pioneers of the movement—
whose memory is revered by all Co-operators—the Rochdale
Pioneers.

It is presumed, therefore, that this was the Co-operation
propounded, for much interest was evinced, causing considerable discussion and questions.   So well satisfied was the
meeting with the proposals that a Provisional Committee
was formed to draw up rules and to make the necessary
arrangements for the taking over of the business of Mr.
Dobson, whose business was grocery (wholesale and retail),
wine and spirit merchant, &c.

The names of the gentlemen forming this Provisional
Committee—who might very well be termed the Society's
pioneers — were :· Messrs. Arthur Cuss, J. W. Callison,
J. Platt, Drinkwater, Joseph Pickvance, W. Hilton
Thompson, Holroyde, J. Hurst, and Mr. John Boys, to act
as Secretary *pro tem.*

It was further resolved to form a Society of Co-operation
in Beswick, at Mr. John Dobson's, 30, Ashton New Road,
Beswick, the Society to be called the " Beswick Co-operative
Society Limited."

A small beginning, truly, but to what dimensions it has
grown will be gleaned from the following pages.

As with all other institutions, the foundations were being
laid, and the Provisional Committee met weekly at Mr.
Dobson's to report progress.

On January 27th the following persons were enrolled the
first members of the new Society : Messrs. Arthur Cuss,
John T. Dobson, Joseph Pickvance, John Boys, J. Platt,
J. Hurst, I. Mullinder, T. S. Dobson, S. B. Ramsbottom, and
J. W. Whalley.

The important duty of drawing up the rules governing the
Society was entrusted to a Sub-Committee composed of
Messrs. Pickvance, Boys, and J. Dobson, and when completed
they were submitted to the Registrar for approval.

This meeting also agreed with Mr. Dobson upon the
terms on which his business was to be purchased, and it is
interesting to note that the fixtures, utensils, rolling stock,

W·H·AXON
LATE AUDITOR

R·S·CLARK
LATE AUDITOR

LATE
COMMITTEEMEN

P·RYDER

A·BORSEY

J·BOYS
LATE SECRETARY

NOTABLE WORKERS

and goodwill were transferred for the sum of £170. The stock, it was estimated, would be about £200, though it was arranged that it should be purchased by valuation. The weekly turnover was stated to be £60, and was managed by Mr. Dobson, who would continue in the Society's service. Up to this date 84 shares were reported to have been taken up.

ESTABLISHMENT.

On June 4th, 1892, the Society became an established fact, duly registered under the Industrial and Provident Societies Act, 1876, the terms of the certificate being as follows :—

ACKNOWLEDGMENT OF REGISTRY OF SOCIETY.

The BESWICK CO-OPERATIVE SOCIETY LIMITED is registered under the Industrial and Provident Societies Act, 1876, this 4th day of June, 1892.

E.W. B.

Copy kept—E.W. B.

The office was registered at 30, Ashton New Road, Beswick, so that, therefore, the business of Mr. John Dobson ceased to exist, and became what was known hereafter the Beswick Co-operative Society Limited.

Upon receipt of the Certificate of Registry the Committee ordered 500 copies of the rules to be printed, along with other stationery ; caused the signs over the shop to receive the name of the Society ; and a seal of the Society, bearing a fluttering bee in the centre of disc, to be made. The seal and various important documents were given into the care of Messrs. Cuss and Dobson. Handbills and posters were issued invit'ng the public to join in the forward movement and to take up shares.

The Society having arrived at something like definiteness and being ready for business, the Committee on June 21st appointed Mr. James Ashhurst Secretary to the Society, his duties to be the preparation of minutes of the meetings held and the keeping of the accounts of the Society, which duties he undertook during his spare hours—another instance of valuable enthusiasm for the progress of this Society.

Business operations commenced on July 1st, a valuation of Mr. Dobson's stock having been made by a representative of the Co-operative Wholesale Society, which amounted to £245, and was taken over by the Society.

A banking account was opened with the Bradford branch of the Joint Stock Bank (now known as the London and Midland Bank), and the Manager and Secretary were empowered to transact the business with the bank.

Membership of the Co-operative Wholesale Society Ltd

On July 26th the Society loyally applied to the Co-operative Wholesale Society Limited to be admitted a member of their institution, twelve shares being requested. In due course the Society was enrolled a member at one of the C.W.S. General Meetings without any opposition, and Mr. Dobson was given the honour of being the Society's first delegate to attend the Quarterly Meeting of the C.W.S. held on September 10th, the Society being entitled to send one representative.

Notably, the Society was also enrolled a member of the Off-Licence Association on August 2nd, being dealers in wines and spirits—a rather strange membership for a Society in the movement—but which, however, lapsed on June 9th, 1896, when the Committee, having for some time considered that it was not in harmony with the principles of thrift to retain their wine and spirit licence, unanimously decided to discontinue the sale of intoxicants in our shops. Lest it should be thought by the members that it was brought about by some bigoted teetotalers, I may add that the resolution was moved and seconded by two gentlemen with very open minds upon the question.

The total sales for the first four weeks of the Society's existence reached £162. 4s. 5d., an average of about £40 per week, and, rapidly growing, the Manager, Mr. Dobson, was compelled to exchange his rolling stock for something more convenient to deal with the collection of goods bought.

First Quarterly Meeting.

Messrs. J. Fletcher and W. H. Axon were appointed on October 25th to audit the first quarter's accounts, which ended on October 5th, and report thereon. A draft of the report and balance sheet was submitted to the Committee for consideration on November 1st, and, being approved, 250 copies were ordered to be printed and circulated.

The Congregational School, Every Street, was engaged for the holding of the first Quarterly Meeting on November 22nd. Mr. Arthur Cuss was voted to the chair. The minutes recorded show evidence of much interest taken by the members present. Many questions were asked, and satisfactorily answered, relative to the encouraging results of the first quarter's transactions, carried through so successfully by the Provisional Committee. It is almost unnecessary to say that the report and balance sheet were adopted unanimously. There were two nominations for the office of President—all officers having to be elected at this meeting—but Mr. Arthur Cuss was elected with a large majority. For the formation of a Committee of Management nine nominations were received for eight positions, and the following gentlemen were elected, but to retire for re-election after the period subjoined to their names : Messrs. J. Hurst and J. Platt (twelve months), G. Poole and J. Ashworth (nine months), J. Ruddock and E. Connell (six months), S. B. Ramsbottom and J. Berry (three months).

Messrs. J. Fletcher and W. H. Axon were appointed Senior and Junior Auditor, respectively, without opposition.

The members evidently, in the initial stages of the Society, had an eye to the social side of life, for they instructed the Committee to arrange, at an early date, a tea party for them at a charge of about 6d. per head.

The Chairman was accorded a hearty vote of thanks for his manner of conducting the meeting.

B

BESWICK CO-OPERATIVE SOCIETY LIMITED.

FIRST QUARTERLY REPORT,

From July 1st to October 5th, 1892.

FIRST OFFICERS:

Manager: Mr. J. T. DOBSON.   *Secretary*: Mr. JAMES ASHHURST.

Auditors: Messrs. JAMES FLETCHER and W. H. AXON.

Committee: Messrs. ARTHUR CUSS, JOSEPH PLATT, J. T. DOBSON, JOHN HURST, T. S. DOBSON, and JOSEPH PICKVANCE.

Bankers: THE LONDON AND MIDLAND BANK LIMITED.

TO THE MEMBERS.

In presenting this, our first Report, we have to congratulate you on the success which has attended the operations of the Society during the first quarter of its existence.

The profits, after making provision for all expenses incidental to trade, are sufficient to pay a dividend of 1s. per £ on members' purchases, in addition to carrying over a considerable balance to next quarter's account, which, we think, will be considered satisfactory.

Seventy-six persons have joined the Society during the quarter, and we would urge on our members the desirability of bringing the Society before the notice of their friends, as we feel sure such a course would greatly benefit the Society (especially if attention was drawn to the quality and the price of our goods) by at once increasing the number of members and enlarging the business, which, of course, would enable us to do even better next quarter.

A statement of the Society's accounts for the past quarter, showing a turnover of £794. 19s. 6½d., is herewith submitted for your approval.

We propose to deal with the profit as follows:—

	£	s.	d.
Dividend on Members' Purchases—£280 at 1s. per £	14	0	0
Interest on Share Capital	3	4	8
Balance carried forward to next Quarter	12	16	8
	£30	1	4

THE QUARTERLY MEETING will be held on TUESDAY, the 22nd NOVEMBER, 1892, at 7-30 p.m., in the INFANTS' ROOM, at the CONGREGATIONAL SCHOOLS, EVERY STREET, MANCHESTER.

Signed, on behalf of the Committee,

JAMES ASHHURST, *Secretary.*

NOTICE.

A person may join the Society at any time on payment of an Entrance Fee of 1s., and 6d. for Pass Book and Rules. Every member is required to hold one £1 share, which may be paid up at once or by instalments of 2s. 6d. per Quarter, and no member can hold more than 200 Shares. All Shares are withdrawable except the first, which is transferable only.

Check Sheets must not be brought in on Friday or Saturday.

DIVIDEND will be paid THURSDAY, NOVEMBER 24th, at the Store. Dividend not withdrawn will be placed to Share Account.

CASH ACCOUNT.

Dr.

	£ s. d.	£ s. d.
To Contributions	£3 16 0	274 7 6
" Entrance Fees	1 18 0	
" Rules		5 14 0
" Sales	794 19 6¼	
Less Accounts owing to Society	31 0 10	763 18 8¼
		£1044 0 2½

Cr.

	£ s. d.	£ s. d.	£ s. d.
By Goods	1002 1 8¼		
" Carriage	0 16 5		
		1002 18 1¾	
Less Accounts owing by Society		270 1 7	
		732 16 6¼	
" Fixtures		170 0 0	
" Expenses—			
Stable Account	4 17 1	16 6 6	
Licences Account			
Printing, Stationery, Advertising, and Postage	22 4 9		
Repairs to Buildings	7 11 9		
Lighting, Heating, &c.	1 12 4		
Wages	37 10 0		
Rent, Rates, and Taxes	15 13 3		
	105 15 8		
Less Accounts owing by Society	6 14 9	99 0 11	
" Co-operative Wholesale Society—Share Account		0 12 0	
" Cash in Bank		19 15 1	
" Cash in hand		21 15 8	
		£1044 0 2½	

EXPENSES ACCOUNT.

	£ s. d.
To General Expenses	105 15 8
	£105 15 8

		£ s. d.
By Amount chargeable to this Quarter		69 19 2
" Suspense Account, or amount to be apportioned on succeeding quarters, viz.:—		
Licences	£12 6 6	
Printing, &c.	11 0 0	
Repairs to Buildings	5 11 9	
Rates	5 0 3	
		33 18 6
" Rules		1 18 0
		£105 15 8

Dr.   FIXED STOCK ACCOUNT.   **Cr.**

	£ s. d.		£ s. d.
To Amount expended	170 0 0	By Entrance Fees	3 16 0
		" Present Nominal Value	166 4 0
	£170 0 0		£170 0 0

TRADE ACCOUNT.

	£ s. d.	£ s. d.		£ s. d.
To Goods	1002 1 8¾		By Sales	794 19 6½
" Carriage	0 16 5	1002 18 1½	" Stock in Trade	307 19 1
" Expenses		69 19 2		
" Balance, or Profit		30 1 4		
		£1102 18 7½		£1102 18 7½

CAPITAL ACCOUNT.

	£ s. d.	£ s. d.		£ s. d.
To Members' Claims	*270 1 7	274 7 6	By Co-operative Wholesale Society – Share	0 12 0
" Trade Accounts owing			" London and Midland Bank	19 5 1
" Expenses Accounts owing	6 14 9		" Amount owing for Goods sold	31 18 10
" Balance, or Profit		276 16 4	" Suspense Account (see Expenses Account)	33 18 6
		30 1 4	" Fixed Stock Account	166 4 0
			" Stock in Trade	307 19 1
			" Balance in hand	21 15 8
		£581 5 2		£581 5 2

* This includes £205 balance owing for the purchase of Mr. Dobson's business and stock.

PROPOSED DISPOSAL OF THE BALANCE.

	£ s. d.		£ s. d.
To Dividend on Members' Purchases, £280 at 1s. in the £	14 0 0	By Balance Profit	30 1 4
" Interest on Members' Claims at 5 per cent per annum	3 4 8		
" Balance carried to next Quarter	12 16 8		
	£30 1 4		£30 1 4

Audited and found correct—JAMES FLETCHER, W. H. AXON, Auditors.

Mr. Arthur Cuss, the first President, has been a resident, and well known, in the neighbourhood for over forty years. He followed well, in the Co-operative movement, his father, who had been a Director of the Manchester and Salford Equitable Co-operative Society for twenty years, and only relinquished that office by his death, the Society erecting a stone over his resting place to his memory. Mr. Cuss was a very active worker for the benefit of this Society, and ever willing to give his time and energy in the furtherance of its objects, and was very proud of the success the Society was attaining. Mr. Cuss acted as substitute for Mr. Dobson, the Manager, in the buying of goods and as general superintendent during the latter's absence for two weeks through illness, without incurring any expense to the Society, having given his services voluntarily.

Mr. Cuss commenced business for himself as printer and stationer some twenty years ago, and has carried on a successful business ever since he laid down his motto, " Deal only in the best," there being plenty of goods otherwise on the market. This motto he adapted, during his tenure of office, to the utmost possibility with the Beswick Co-operative Society Limited.

The Committee, determined to keep acquainted with the doings of the parent body, the Co-operative Wholesale Society, again appointed their Manager to attend the Quarterly Meeting to be held on December 10th, and sufficient to record that delegates have been continuously appointed to every meeting up to the present time, both from the Committee and from the members, as the Society's representation grew. It is also interesting to note that the first dividend received from the C.W.S. was 10s. 5d., a rate of 2½d. per £ on purchases of £50— rather different from what it is at the present day.

A new kind of business was indirectly introduced into the Society's operations on December 6th with the supply of boots and shoes to members by a local tradesman on commission, the Society allowing full dividend on purchases.

ARTHUR CUSS.

G. E. STOTT.

LATE PRESIDENTS.

CHAPTER II.

—

1893.

THE first members' annual tea party was held on February 8th, and took place in the Congregational Schools, Every Street, the Manager and a Sub-Committee having made all arrangements. It proved a very successful gathering, though, as with all such gatherings, a small loss was sustained. It is a point with this Society to always give the members the best of everything, so that it is impossible to make profit out of the events. The idea of arranging these features is not so much for the accumulation of profit, but to provide the means of social intercourse and the brightening of otherwise monotonous lives. The minutes onward are almost congested with reference to arrangements for tea parties, and the events, being of such great importance, seemingly, cannot be rushed. Everyone enjoys tea parties, but it never enters one's mind what an amount of time and worry they occasion to make them successful.

The business of the Society continued to grow so rapidly that additional staff had to be engaged, and the Committee, desirous of supplying the members with all their requirements, though which could only be done gradually, arranged with local tradespeople to supply them with millinery, drapery, and clothing on commission, the Society allowing full dividend on those purchases.

The second Quarterly Meeting was held on February 28th, and this date was subsequently recognised as the Annual General Meeting, at which the election of the President takes place. Messrs. J. Nuttall and J. T. Blease were elected on the Committee, and so changed the constitution of the first Committee. The Auditors, upon the recommendation of the Committee, were granted the sum of 10s. 6d. each per quarter in recognition of their services until further notice, having up to now given their services for the benefit of the Society. The Committee received instructions from the members to introduce some form of club for weekly subscriptions, so that they could purchase goods other than groceries. This was duly inaugurated later by the Manager.

Unfortunately, on April 11th one of the pioneers of the Society, Mr. J. Hurst, tendered his resignation as a member of the Committee, which was accepted with regret. The vacancy was filled at the next Quarterly Meeting in the person of Mr. J. Knowles, along with two other changes on the Committee by the election of Messrs. J. Hall and W. Taplin. Many changes seem to have taken place in the constitution of the Committee during the year, for Messrs. Frost and Borsey secured places at the fourth Quarterly Meeting. The accounts for the fourth quarter were audited by Mr. Abraham Haigh, accountant, owing to indisposition of the Auditors.

At the end of the first twelve months the business of the Society recorded sales, £3,583. 4s. 8½d. ; membership, 147 ; dividend paid, £124. 4s. ; interest on capital, £17. 3s. 2d. ; share capital, £456. 12s. 10d.

Membership of the Co-operative Union Limited.

A deputation from the Manchester District Association of the Co-operative Union Limited waited upon the Committee on September 5th with the object of inducing the Society to become members of the Co-operative Union Limited, drawing attention to the advantages to be derived by being members thereof. The Society, it was pointed out, would be entitled to send two delegates to the Annual Congress ; to obtain gratuitous advice from the Union solicitor on law matters ; speakers for public meetings supplied ; assistance given in audits and kindred matters ; and mutual aid and counsel. The Committee unanimously decided to make application to be enrolled a member, and to subscribe to the funds our due proportion in accordance with their rules. Our application was duly welcomed by the Co-operative Union, and we were forthwith enrolled a loyal member without question.

The reader should bear in mind the foregoing paragraph, and likewise the paragraph on page 16 relating to the admission of the Society as a member of the Co-operative Wholesale Society, when considering the phases that arise in the discussions of amalgamation and boundary lines chronicled later in this history, which may probably be viewed in a different aspect otherwise.

At this period our district was in the throes of a miners' strike, universal amongst the collieries in Lancashire. About 500 persons were affected in our neighbourhood, and consequently the Society's business suffered to a considerable extent. The C.W.S. allocated £10, out of £5,000 voted by their members to relieve distress, to this Society, which was distributed by the Committee in goods.

On October 3rd, Mr. Nuttall, a member of the Committee, tendered his resignation, owing to his work interfering with the duties, which was received with regret. The vacancy was filled later by Mr. Nightingale. Mr. Nuttall, however, found himself able to resume his duties when re-elected on November 27th, 1894.

A note in the Committee's report for the fifth quarter is worthy of repetition, and might be again emphasised :—

In response to our appeal to bring the Society under the notice of their friends, a number of our members have done excellent work, some having introduced four new members during the quarter, and we should like each member to try and do likewise, when we should soon have one of the most flourishing Societies in the kingdom.

It was little thought, no doubt, when this paragraph was written that in so short a lapse of time their ambitions should be maturing, and that, at the end of fifteen years, the Society should be in a position to present a History of nothing but progression. The Society is now one of the most flourishing and well known Societies in the movement, and at the present rate of progress will be enabled at the end of another fifteen years to place more interesting facts before the notice of the members.

First Branch.

The Committee now thought it was opportune to extend their business operations by placing a branch in the Ancoats

district.   Investigations were instituted, with the result that
on December 19th power was vested in the Manager and Chairman to secure the shop and premises situate at the corner of
Mill Street and Carruthers Street on a tenancy, if, after
inspection, they considered they would be suitable for the
Society's business.   They decided to take a tenancy of the
premises, purchasing the fixtures for the nominal sum of £6.
A lease for three years at the annual rent of £24 was agreed to.
Therefore, Branch No. 1 was opened for business on Friday,
January 25th, 1894, Mr. T. H. Martin being appointed to
manage it.   A large number of handbills were circulated
announcing the opening.

1894.

Another Committee-man, Mr. Knowles, was compelled to
tender his resignation on January 23rd, owing to his removal
from Manchester, which was accepted with regret, though he
had only held office a short period.   There is no doubt that to
lose the services of a Committee-man who has filled office for
some length of time, and thereby gained experience and knowledge of the Society's business, must have some influence on
the Society's progression, and, therefore, it is regrettable
when such losses are experienced.   It is well instanced in
many members of the Society's present Committee, who have
held office for a good number of years (some thirteen years),
and have done yeoman service, much of the success of the
Society being attributable to their early efforts.   New
officers have always to adapt themselves before they can feel
to be of service, and, therefore, they generally are deprecated.

COMMITTEE'S REMUNERATION.

Up to now the Committee had generously given their
services for the benefit of the Society, but at the Quarterly
Meeting held on February 27th the members cordially resolved
to recognise their services in the shape of an annual grant of
10s. per head, which sum, it was suggested, should be spent
on an annual picnic, and that those persons who had served
on the Committee at any time during the twelve months

FIRST SHOP OPENED
MILL ST., ANCOATS.

BESWICK COOPERATIVE SOCIETY Ltd
DRAPERY, BOOT, TAILORING DEPARTMENT.

FIRST DRAPERY
AND BOOT SHOP

BESWICK COOPERATIVE SOCIETY Ltd
BUTCHERING DEPARTMENT.

BUTCHERING DEPT.
142, ASHTON NEW Rd BESWICK.

immediately preceding the date on which the picnic takes place should be eligible for invitation. The Manager, Secretary, and Auditors were incorporated in the resolution.

I venture to suggest that it was not a very handsome reward for the valuable services rendered, but evidently the result of their labour was sufficient reward and encouragement.

The business of the Society was growing to such an extent that the Committee were compelled to take into consideration the question of either enlarging their present Central or securing more suitable premises. They, therefore, set themselves the task, and, though it appears so easy in saying so on paper, it was found to be no light one, and, verily, the fore-runner of many difficulties to be experienced. In making investigations in the district it was suggested that the premises, 70, Ashton New Road, and two shops adjoining, could be purchased from Mr. Wainwright for about £1,200, subject to an annual chief rent of about £12.

The reader will probably gather that the Society was becoming soundly established from the fact that the Committee were concerned about the investment of about £400 lying at the bank in excess of the business requirements. It was thought desirable to invest it with the C.W.S. on deposit at 4 per cent, but they were unsuccessful in their endeavour owing to such account being closed.

The Committee appeared to have their hands full about August, for it was also found necessary to provide further accommodation at the branch premises, Mill Street. The tenant of an adjoining cottage somewhat solved the difficulty by offering his front room and cellar, with the landlord's consent, for the rental of £3 per annum. This method being more advantageous to the Society than by giving notice to the Society's house tenant to quit, thus losing revenue, the Committee closed with the offer, and arrangements to properly secure the connection of the extension against intrusion were agreed to.

Several items of importance were discussed at the Quarterly Meeting on November 27th. A question was raised by Mr. J. H. Chadwick on the manner of taking stock, stating that a member of the Committee ought to be present at the stocktakings and certify the correctness of the quantities entered. It was decided to adopt this course in future, and that the Stocktaker should receive 2s. 6d. for his services. This course has been acted upon up to the present day.

The first subscription, £1. 1s., to the Ancoats Hospital was voted at this meeting, thereby showing the desire to contribute to charitable objects when able to do so ; proving also that the principle of Co-operation is something more than mere trade. A Co-operative Society is nothing if not truly sympathetic with the objects of charitable institutions existing for the benefit of poor people unable to provide themselves with medical assistance or specialists. This subscription has since been gradually increased to £10. 10s. per annum, and many other grants, donations, and subscriptions are generously voted annually by the members to various institutions.

An unusual resolution was also carried at this meeting, showing the goodwill of the members, and read :—" That a cordial vote of thanks be given to the Chairman, Committee, officers, and employés of the Society for their services during the past quarter."

The number of employés at this date was seven.

1895.

The Committee during this year were subject to many anxious moments, and, despite the fact that they were desirous of securing more suitable Central premises, the present accommodation being too limited, received notice from the landlord on January 3rd that the rent of the Central premises would be increased in June next to £40 per annum. It was thereupon decided to ask the landlord if he would sell same to them, together with the adjoining shop. The reply came in the negative, as he had no desire whatever to part with the buildings, so that the only course left open was to pay the increased rent, tantamount to an imposition, or secure other property.

A price was, however, obtained from Mr. Wainwright of property recently offered, namely, £350 for either 70 or 72,

Ashton New Road, the two subject to an annual chief rent of £13. 10s. We could also lease the cellar and house part of No. 68 for five years at 5s. per week.

Though other inquiries were instituted for suitable property in the neighbourhood, nothing could be secured until December, when the premises at 70, Ashton New Road, became vacant, and we were accepted as tenants on lease at a rental of £38 per annum by Mr. Wainwright, with the house and cellar parts of No. 68. It was outside the Committee's ability at this period either to purchase or build Central premises, owing to the want of sufficient capital. The landlord of the present Central premises was unreasonable in his demands for stipulations regarding our tenancy, and, though he pretended that he would not mind losing our tenancy, he was very concerned to retain us, offering various concessions when he saw we were determined to secure more suitable premises. It was a matter of twelve months' worry to the officials, this seeking of fresh Central premises, and it was a relief when the above were secured.

On April 2nd a member of the Committee, Mr. Nightingale, was compelled to tender his resignation owing to having obtained an appointment abroad ; and the Committee, in accepting same with sincere regrets at losing his valuable services, congratulated him on having secured the appointment, and wished him success with his labour in another country.

In May the Committee received an offer of property for extension of business, and were favourably disposed to consider it, viz., two shops and two cottages, situate at the corner of Ashton New Road and Parker Street, Bradford, at a price of £900, subject to an annual chief of £3. The Secretary, however, drew attention to Rule 15, which forbade the contracting of any loan for more than half of the Society's declared capital, and that, therefore, the Society's borrowing powers were limited to £400 or £500. The offer was considered by the Committee to be a desirable position for a branch, but the terms were beyond consideration, so that it was decided to try and obtain better terms.

C

C.W.S. EMPLOYEES.

Many items of note transpired during the year under review, conspicuous amongst which was the following, which I purpose to treat at length owing to the addition having played such an important part in the history and progress of the Society, and to the stability with which the Society has eventually risen, which redounds considerably to the credit of those who first introduced it.

On May 9th the Secretary received the following letter, which was submitted to the Committee :—

C.W.S., Balloon Street,

Manchester, *May 7th, 1895.*

DEAR SIR,

      Mr. Connor had some conversation with your Mr. Dobson on Tuesday last *re* the employés here. In continuation of this, can you call your Committee together to-morrow (Thursday) evening to meet a deputation on the question? If convenient, we will wait upon you from 8-15 to 8-30.

Yours truly,

(Signed) B. TETLOW, General Office.

The deputation, consisting of Messrs. Tetlow, Fenton, and Connor, introduced by Mr. J. H. Chadwick, was received by the Committee, who submitted the following details for consideration: Up to recently the employés at the C.W.S. had been privileged to purchase any goods there for their use and consumption at wholesale prices, but at the last Quarterly Meeting the delegates had decided to withdraw this privilege. This decision, of course, meant a considerable pecuniary loss to the employés, inasmuch as it caused them to have to pay the ordinary retail price at some outside establishment for goods which they had been in the habit of purchasing at the C.W.S., and it had not been accompanied by any increase of remuneration. With the view of, as far as possible, restoring the privilege, the employés had decided to ask this Committee if they were prepared to allow these purchases to be made in the name of the Society; and, if so, upon what terms? The sales to employés during the past twelve months, including the grocery department, amounted to upwards of £9,000, and in support of their application they made various suggestions to the Committee as to the manner in which the business could be conducted.

At the close of the foregoing statement the members of the deputation were interrogated by the Committee on several points in connection with the subject, who, however, stated they were unable to say whether the employés interested would be willing to become members of this Society in the ordinary way.

It was, however, resolved at a subsequent meeting of the Committee, " That, while this Society is open to receive the C.W.S. employés as ordinary members, it cannot offer to them any exceptional facilities as regards their purchases." The Secretary was instructed to communicate this decision to the C.W.S. employés.

An arrangement must have been made subsequently for the employés to make their purchases through this Society, for it is recorded that the Manager undertook for a considerable period the collection of the accounts on behalf of the Society from the C.W.S. employés who had become members. They have remained consistently loyal to this Society up to the present day, in spite of tempting offers from other Societies, and their business has so developed that it is a department in itself, managed by two clerks, with a turnover of about £17,000 per annum.

CHAPTER III.

Parker Street Property.

ON May 14th it was reported that the lowest possible price that would be accepted for the purchase of the two shops and the two cottages at the corner of Parker Street and Ashton New Road, which had a present gross rental of £49 per annum, was £600, subject to a yearly chief of £3, or £750, free from chief, the property being freehold. It was thereupon decided to ask Mr. Tunstall to make a valuation of the property, and to call a Special Meeting of the members for May 28th to consider the following resolution :—

That, having regard to the Society's urgent need for more commodious premises, on account of the increasing business at its Ashton New Road shop, and recognising the great difficulty there is in acquiring a suitable shop or plot of land in the neighbourhood, this meeting, with the view of offering every facility to the Committee of Management in their efforts to obtain, by purchase or otherwise, convenient premises or land, hereby empowers them to enter into such arrangement and expenditure, compatible with the Society's rules, as they may deem to the Society's interest, without further appeal or reference to the general members of the Society by way of Special Meeting or otherwise.

This resolution was unanimously agreed to at that meeting, with the following condition appended :—

That it be distinctly understood that the operation of this resolution is confined strictly to the Society's present want, and that when purchasing property at any future time the Committee shall apply to the general body of members before completing the negotiations.

Following upon this permission, and having obtained several expert opinions that the price of £750 free from chief for the property at the corner of Parker Street was extremely reasonable, it was resolved unanimously by the Committee :—

That the offer of two shops and two cottages, situate at the corner of Parker Street and Ashton New Road, for the sum of £750, free from chief—the property being freehold—be and is hereby accepted, and that, when necessary, a cheque on the Society's bankers be duly drawn and signed for the amount of deposit required.

No. 3 BRANCH, PARKER STREET, BRADFORD.
(Second Branch Opened.)

The deeds were duly drawn up and sealed, and the property passed into the possession of the Society.   It was thereupon decided to depreciate the property at the rate of 5 per cent per annum.   The Society thus became property owners for the first time with this acquisition.

It was not until late in September that the premises were opened for the transaction of business.   Handbills were freely circulated announcing the opening of No. 2 Branch, Parker Street.   Consequently there was a large influx of new members—about 100—and the trade was assured.

To celebrate the opening a visit of inspection of the C.W.S. premises, Balloon Street, was arranged, and tea provided for the members, the party journeying by conveyances.

DELEGATES' EXPENSES.

Up to June 25th the Committee's representatives to various conferences and meetings had been without any allowances for out-of-pocket expenses, but this it was decided to remedy by arranging that in future any delegate representing this Society at any conference or meeting outside Manchester should be allowed third-class railway fare and 1s. for incidental expenses out of the funds of the Society.   This, in my opinion, is as it should be, though hardly sufficient inducement for any delegate to devote his leisure in the interests of the Society; but may be, of course, somewhat different when the delegates appointed have the interests of the Society at heart.   This remuneration was, however, increased later, which will be recorded in due course.

Arrangements were made in October with the Coal Supply Association to supply our members with coal, who allowed a sufficient margin of profit for the payment of dividend on the trade.   The Bradford Colliery Company had also made a similar arrangement.

A branch of the Manchester and Liverpool District Bank having been opened in close proximity to our Central premises, it was decided on November 12th to transfer our banking business to it, the terms of business being similar to our present bankers'.   It was also decided to empower the

Manager to sign cheques, bills, and other documents having
reference to the banking business, without being countersigned by the Secretary—rather an unusual proceeding, and
I would suggest unbusinesslike—for the sake of convenience.
For the security of the Manager's fidelity the Committee had
a deed drawn up granting the Society a lien on the Manager's
share account of £200.

AMALGAMATION.

Now that the Society had attained something like recog-
nisable proportions, and continuing to make rapid progress
after about four years' struggle (though, perhaps, not serious)
to put it into a sound financial condition, overtures were
instituted on the subject of amalgamation. No exception
had been taken, you must fully understand, at the registration
of the Society in the first instance; no objection to the application for admission as members of the parent body—the
Co-operative Wholesale Society—in the second instance;
and, in the third instance, we were even approached by an
influential body in the Manchester Co-operative world to
induce us to become members of the Co-operative Union
Limited; each of which was taken up with unanimity and a
loyal spirit to the movement.   Yet, paradoxical as it may
seem, the Committee were waited upon on December
3rd by a deputation from the Co-operative Union Limited,
consisting of Messrs. Hardern and Watson, who stated that
the Manchester and Salford Society had requested the Union
to enter into negotiations with this Society with the view of
ascertaining if terms could not be arranged for the amalgamation of the two Societies, as it was felt the carrying out of such
a scheme would be for the ultimate benefit of all parties concerned, and would, of course, obviate any possible competition
between the Societies in question. Failing amalgamation,
the Union suggested that a line of demarcation should be
mutually agreed upon, mapping out the respective districts of
the two Societies, with the understanding that neither Society
in its operations should encroach beyond the boundary line
into the neighbour's district.

After making this statement, and receiving general
information respecting this Society's formation, growth, and

present position, the gentlemen forming the deputation were informed that the question would receive the fullest and most careful consideration, and, when a decision was arrived at, it would be transmitted to the Co-operative Union. It was eventually deferred for the purpose of laying the question before the members at the next Quarterly Meeting.

The books are inundated with references to the amalgamation and boundary line questions even up to the present day, and it is, therefore, impossible at this juncture to relate the whole of the details appertaining to it. I, therefore, crave the indulgence of the reader to the various passages, as they occur, indicative of the progress made, and the attitude taken up, upon this question, at the same time placing before you our true position.

" WHEATSHEAF."

On December 10th the C.W.S. decided to publish a monthly record of events connected with their business and the movement generally, which they intended to christen the " Wheatsheaf." They invited Societies, by a specimen copy, to take up space of two or more pages for local items of interest, and to place an order for copies to distribute amongst the members. The Committee decided to take advantage of an offer that would supply a long-felt want, and which has since been the means of conveying a mass of information and many items of interest to our members. The first issue took place on July 1st, 1896, this Society ordering 500 copies for distribution to its members gratis, and placed the responsibility for supplying the local information upon the Chairman for the time being.

1896.

The year just reviewed was abounding with many details that provide materials for history, but the one we now open with was a very eventful one to this Society. Many changes were made, and extensions to the Society's operations, to which due reference will be given. The foundations having been laid by the pioneers, duly recorded in the foregoing pages, it remains now simply a matter of placing on record the remarkable progress the Society has achieved.

C.W.S. EMPLOYEES.

Some misunderstanding appears to have arisen in regard to the way in which the C.W.S. employes' trade should be carried on. The Committee had the matter under their consideration, and it was resolved :—

That, inasmuch as there appears to have been some ground for misunderstanding by a portion of those members of this Society who are C.W.S. employés as to the terms upon which they were admitted, such of them as desire it may, upon application, have their shares bought in by the Society at the full sum standing to the credit of the shareholder when the sale is effected.

A circular was issued to this effect, but as a result only one member withdrew his share and shortly afterwards rejoined.

Later on in the year, however, a Special Meeting of the members was called for the purpose of considering the following resolutions :—

1. That it is injurious to the interests of this Society that employés of the Co-operative Wholesale Society Limited sit upon the Committee, and that this meeting call upon them to resign.

2. That this meeting proceed to elect two persons to fill their places.

The meeting was held with Mr. Bowden in the chair, and, though the resolutions were challenged as not being in accordance with the Society's rules, they were put and defeated by a large majority.

At the meeting of the Committee following the Special General Meeting Mr. Stott raised the question relating to the C.W.S. employés, and expressed regret at the unfortunate differences that were existent. He suggested, with a view to the settlement of the whole matter, that this Committee appoint three members to confer with three representatives of the employés upon the position generally, to arrive at some amicable understanding.

Messrs. Chadwick, Kayton, Bowden, Connor, and Howarth, however, met the whole of the Committee on May 15th and made certain suggestions, and as a result of long and careful deliberation the Committee agreed to the suggestions in their entirety.

This, therefore, ended all further friction between this section of the Society's members, and they have since proved to be a very valuable support to the Society by the large addition to the membership, their continued loyalty, their capital, and a trade which has now reached to about £17,000 per annum.

A city office was opened in November for the transaction of this particular business in Dantzic Street, near to Balloon Street, but has since been transferred to Corporation Street, where attendance is given three days per week.

Canvassing at Elections.

There appeared to be some anxious moments for the retiring members of the Committee, who were deeply concerned about the result of the forthcoming election at the February Quarterly Meeting, and, to promote their candidature, had handbills printed, but took the liberty of placing them upon the shop counters, giving instructions to the shopmen to distribute them amongst the members. Another member of the Committee, who saw them and considered the action a wrong one, confiscated them until after the election.

These two gentlemen evidently intended not to be outwitted, for they had another quantity printed, but with an additional paragraph stating that this handbill was issued on February 21st, but was stolen, so they had, therefore, reissued it. Whether it was again placed upon the counters I know not. Anyhow, one of the retiring members was defeated at the poll, and then the question was raised in Committee. At a subsequent meeting the following resolution was adopted:—

That, in future, no handbills in favour of the candidature of any person or persons for seats on the Committee be allowed to be placed in the Society's shops for distribution to the members except by the sanction and permission of the Committee.

It was also further resolved :—

That any employé canvassing votes on the Society's premises for the election of any member for a seat on the Committee of Management will be severely dealt with, and that cards be printed containing this caution, and that this notice be posted in the grocery departments at the same time as nomination papers, and only taken down after the Quarterly Meeting has been held.

It also appeared that there had been no supervision, up to the present, of the attendance of members at Quarterly Meetings, but it was decided to remedy this state of things by the issue of admission cards to members for production at future meetings of the Society, and which would act as a check on the voting in the various elections that take place.

AUDITORS' SALARY.

The duties of the Auditors had so increased that a member of the Committee drew attention to the fact at one of their meetings that they were insufficiently paid with 10s. 6d. each for their services, and it was thereupon decided to recommend the members to increase the Auditors' remuneration to £1 each per quarter.   This recommendation was adopted at the February meeting.   It was also resolved to pay the Committee for their services 1s. per meeting attended (to include Sub-Committee meetings) in lieu of the annual picnic allowed hitherto.

AMALGAMATION.

It was at this Quarterly Meeting that Messrs. Gray and Watson, of the Co-operative Union, attended with the express intention of obtaining the consent of the members to allow the Committee to negotiate with the Manchester and Salford Society for amalgamation.   When, however, the subject was introduced it was obvious that the members had prejudged the question, so it was deemed advisable to test the matter, and from the body of the meeting it was moved, seconded, and resolved unanimously: " That the question of amalgamation be not entertained."   The deputation thereupon addressed a few words to the meeting, and were afterwards accorded a cordial vote of thanks for their presence.   Notwithstanding this decision, the Committee were again approached on the question relative to our neighbouring Societies; and, seeing the question of amalgamation was impossible, a suggestion was made by a deputation from the Co-operative Union on August 4th to the Committee that we should agree to a line of demarcation being drawn limiting our area.   The boundary was to be arranged at a conference of the Manchester and Salford, Failsworth, and Droylsden Societies and ourselves.   The Committee would not, however, give any consideration to the suggestion until some idea of the boundary proposed was submitted.

OLD CENTRAL, 70, ASHTON NEW ROAD, BESWICK.
(Now No. 1 Branch.)

MANAGEMENT.

During the year the Committee made various changes in their mode of business. For instance, on March 3rd it was decided that it was not expedient for any individual member of the Committee to pay a visit of inspection to any of the Society's shops in his capacity as an individual member of the Committee, but that in future the duty of inspection be left in the hands of a Visiting Committee, consisting of two members of the General Committee, to be appointed quarterly, and to report from time to time.

It was also decided that it was time stricter supervision should be exercised over the drawing of cheques, &c., and the banking business generally, the consideration of which was left to the Finance Sub-Committee, who decided that in future, from May 5th, cheques drawn on the Society's banking account must bear the signatures of two members of the Finance Sub-Committee, countersigned by the Manager.

On June 9th the Manager was instructed to purchase all goods in future from the C.W.S., excepting horse provender, bread, and coal, which could not be purchased there; and to see that the tea bought from the C.W.S. was given due prominence in the Society's shops for sale in the ordinary way instead of keeping it in the background as at present, which gives one the impression that the Manager was not in sympathy with the business of the C.W.S.

For the benefit of the members generally it was decided at the Quarterly Meeting held on May 26th that an epitomised report of the Committee's proceedings shall be read in future at each Quarterly Meeting. This, no doubt, keeps the members fully acquainted with the doings of the Committee, and such reports have been given up to the present time.

Various alterations having been carried out at the above premises, the headquarters were transferred there, and opened for business on Thursday, June 4th, a peculiar coincidence with the date of establishment.

With the inception of the new Boardroom in these premises a desirable change was made for the better comfort of the

Committee, which was highly appreciated; so much so that the Chairman, at the first meeting, invited all the officials to tea to celebrate the event, though I am given to understand it took place after the business was transacted, and the evening ended most pleasantly. Up to this removal the meetings had been held under widely different conditions, and it is said that it was most amusing to see members of the Committee endeavouring to balance themselves upon cheese and other boxes; others trying to find more comfort upon bags of sugar or rice, and occasionally the business was interspersed with the variation of a mouse taking a flying leap amongst the goods, with the cat upsetting everything in pursuit. This, with a small kitchen table on which to transact the business, gives a slight idea of the previous constitution of their Boardroom. One would think that a Committee having such important business to deal with deserved better treatment than that meted out to them. But they had to be thankful for mercies, however small.

SECRETARY.

It was at this first meeting in the new Boardroom that Mr. Ashhurst stated that he regretted being compelled to ask the Committee to relieve him of the office of Secretary to the Society, as the work was becoming too heavy for him in conjunction with his permanent occupation. This intimation was received with deep regret, which meant a severance of continuous service since establishment; but the only alternative was to receive it, at the same time expressing their appreciation of his past services, and to consider a new appointment.

It was thought desirable, seeing the business warranted, to secure the services of a permanent Secretary, to devote the whole of his time to the duties of the office and to undertake the financial transactions of the Society. With this object in view an advertisement was inserted in the papers, and from a large number of applicants three gentlemen were selected for interview. Out of these Mr. A. E. Worswick, who had had some years' experience as Assistant Secretary to the York Equitable Industrial Society, was unanimously appointed, on June 26th, Secretary to this Society.

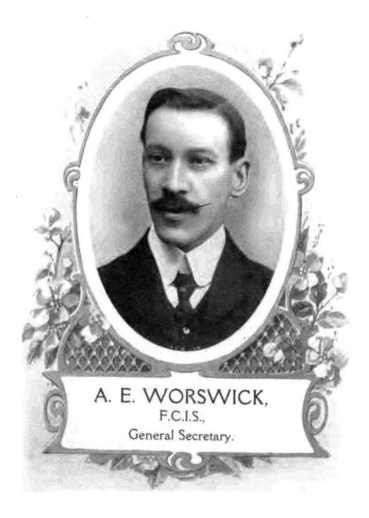

A. E. WORSWICK,
F.C.I.S.,
General Secretary.

D

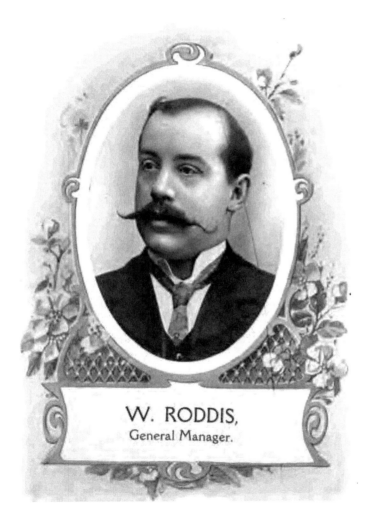

W. RODDIS,
General Manager.

With the advent of a permanent Secretary followed a reorganisation of some portion of the business.   The whole of the books, cash takings, and banking business were placed in his charge as Cashier, as well as Secretary, so that the Manager was relieved of many duties, which gave him more time for supervision.   The check system was also placed under his care, to put it on a basis satisfactory to the Committee—the system being the Eccles system, with gum sheet.   The Secretary was also guaranteed for a large sum for his fidelity.

MANAGER.

The Manager, unfortunately, did not take kindly to this new system, and appeared to feel his position usurped, which was not so, as the Secretary had endeavoured to work amicably with his colleague ; and it was only with the utmost difficulty that the new order of things was instituted.   It was with regret that the Committee, after a lapse of about a month, through the determined conservative manner of the Manager in regard to the new arrangements, found themselves in the predicament of being without a Manager, and had to secure a gentleman to fill the vacancy.   Mr. Cuss, the President, took charge of the business and general super-vision until the new appointment was made.   An advertise-ment was inserted in the papers for a General Manager, and, although there was a large number of applicants, the Committee could not find a better person to fill the vacancy than Mr. W. Roddis, who was the Manager of Parker Street Branch and an applicant, so that he was unanimously appointed on August 27th the Society's General Manager.

The Committee also made an important decision, viz., to discontinue the employment of female labour in connection with our grocery departments, and, in consequence, the services of the lady who had charge of the Mill Street Branch were dispensed with.

The first Members' Picnic was held on July 25th, by 'bus to Heatley Warburton, near Lymm, on which occasion the shops of the Society were closed at 12-30 noon and the employés took advantage of the opportunity by joining the

party.   Many picnics have been held in after years, some by
'bus and some by train, but it has never been found possible
to close the business as on the first occasion.

DRAPERY AND BOOTS.

Following upon the appointment of the Secretary and
Manager, the Committee began to consider the desirability
of extending the Society's operations by providing a grocery
shop in the vicinity of Donkey Common, Ardwick, to cater
for the large population springing up ; one towards South
Street, Openshaw ; and to introduce the business of drapery,
boots, and tailoring at the earliest possible opportunity.

A shop suitable for drapery was secured at 235, Ashton New
Road, Beswick, a lease of tenancy arranged, and a gentleman
engaged as Manager and Buyer for the department.   The
main feature of the business was drapery, but a small stock
of boots and tailoring was added, with a view of nursing the
business until it was opportune to open separately.

The new venture saw light on November 2nd, and has
since continued to be a source of convenience to the members, though it might have received more loyalty from the
members generally ;   still, it now appears to be greatly
improving.   Early in the following year the trade of this
nature done on commission was discontinued, as was also
millinery.   The photo shown on page 29 is the shop in which
the new business was commenced.

The Committee reduced the hours of the various places of
business on November 14th from ten o'clock to nine o'clock on
Saturday evenings.

It was arranged on November 10th for a local tradesman to
supply on commission our members with beef, mutton, &c.,
full dividend on purchases being allowed.   By this means
some trade was got together preliminary to commencing in the
business ourselves.   This arrangement, however, only lasted
about three months, the tradesman finding he could not continue the trade and allow us the commission.

CHAPTER IV.

1897.

On January 12th the Committee, with an idea to still further extend our operations, issued a reply circular to our members, asking if they were in favour of the Society commencing a milk business, and to state the quantity they were prepared to take from us in the event of the result justifying the commencement. Attached to the same circular was a statement by the Committee to the effect that they were desirous of doing a larger coal business amongst our members, the present system being, in their opinion, unsatisfactory, and requested them to say, if bags were introduced instead of having to take a load, how many they would take weekly. The response to the suggestion of a milk business undoubtedly spelt failure, so that the idea was abandoned; but in regard to the new arrangement for the coal business the Committee were inundated with orders for bags weekly, and so arrangements were made forthwith with a local tradesman to supply us with coal in bags and do the carting of same to our members.

The purchase of additional horseflesh is, from experience, as difficult as the buying of land, and after many attempts to secure a horse, having only one at present to cope with the increasing requirements of cartage, one was secured for the sum of £28. Year by year we have had to keep adding to our stables for the purpose of cartage, till now we possess over twelve different kinds of horses. If you were to ask our Manager whether he likes horse buying he would no doubt give you an emphatic " No ! " for, as he says, " Buying a horse is like taking a chance in a lottery—you never know how it will turn out." A nice-looking horse, for which a heavy price is asked, when submitted to the veterinary for examination has some blemish found to destroy its purchase. Then another animal has to be found for the same scrutiny. Our veterinary says, perhaps for our consolation, that he has never yet seen a horse without faults.

BUTCHERING.

From the purchase of horseflesh the Committee had to turn their attention to the necessity of providing a Butchering Department, seeing that the arrangements made with the local tradesman had terminated almost abruptly, to retain what trade had thus been got together. A shop at 142, Ashton New Road, was offered to us ready for starting business, with one or two small alterations, and secured, a tenancy lease being arranged. The shop was opened for business on February 12th, with Mr. C. H. Lees, of Hurst, as Buyer and Manager, which position he still occupies. The opening of this department proved a great convenience to our members, but it has experienced many ups and downs, but now I think it is on a firmer basis.

RULES.

The members, in Quarterly Meeting held on February 23rd, decided to have the rules of the Society revised and brought up to date, and for this purpose a Sub-Committee was formed, consisting of three members of the Board and three from the general body of members. Messrs. Cuss, Brooks, Chadwick, Ashhurst, Bowden, and Kayton formed the Rules Revision Committee, and their work was long and onerous. After revising the rules, amongst which, at the desire of the Committee, a clause was inserted for the meetings of the Committee to be held on Mondays instead of Tuesdays, they were submitted to a Special Meeting of the members on July 16th, who approved them after making one or two alterations. The new rules were registered, the certificate of same being received on September 13th, and a quantity was ordered to be printed for circulation.

The Committee, on March 8th, decided to transfer the banking account from the Manchester and Liverpool District Bank to the Co-operative Wholesale Society's Bank, but arrangements were made for deposits to be still passed through the former bank for the convenience of the Society. This has been a distinct advantage to the Society, as not only are the transactions dealt with on the same terms, but the Society, by being members of the C.W.S., participates in the surplus dividend.

No. 4 BRANCH, 104 RYLANCE STREET, ARDWICK.

EMPLOYEES' PICNIC.

It was on May 3rd that the Committee first generously granted to the employés, who numbered twenty, the privilege of having a full day's holiday on which to hold their annual excursion, and a sum of 3s. per head towards the expenses of those joining the party, which grant subsequently received the approval of the members.   Consequently the employés took advantage of the kindness, and visited Southport on June 16th.   This generosity of the Committee and members has become an annual feature, and is highly appreciated by the employés, which so materially assists their pleasure.

Delegate appointed on various deputations had up to now only received 1s. for their sacrifice of time in the service of the Society, but it was decided on June 8th that in future they should receive a fee of 2s. 6d. in consideration.

Messrs. Macdonald Limited, Piccadilly, arranged in August to supply our members with artificial teeth ; also Messrs. Cowan and Sons, Market Place, to supply eyeglasses and spectacles.   The Society allows full dividend on purchases made from either firm.

ENGINEERS' STRIKE.

The engineers' strike in July caused the sales of the Society to remain somewhat at a standstill, and much distress was experienced for many months in our district—in fact, one might say it was felt for years.   The Society placed £10 for distribution amongst the distressed labourers locked out through the strike, as they had no funds of their own, and this sum was augmented with £25 from the Co-operative Wholesale Society. Many cases of absolute distress came before the notice of the Committee, and were relieved with goods from our shops.   It was extremely gratifying when the termination of the duel was reached for the sake of the distressed.

LAND AND BUILDINGS.

At the Quarterly Meeting held on August 23rd three members, Messrs. Bowden, Kayton, and Roberts, were appointed to work in conjunction with the Board of Management for the purchase of land, endowed with power to purchase a suitable plot. They made several and various inquiries, and their efforts were ultimately rewarded by the purchase of three shops and a cottage from Mr. Wainwright, one tenanted by us on lease at 70, Ashton New Road, and the adjoining property of 68, 72, and 73, Brewery Street. The area of the plot was about 241 square yards, with frontage to the main road. The price paid was £1,350, and subject to a yearly chief of £13. The seal of the Society was affixed to the conveyance prepared by our solicitors on October 18th, and to the deeds when completed, which were handed to our bankers for safe keeping.

SHOP—RYLANCE STREET DISTRICT.

Having settled another important question, the Committee again considered the desirability of extending the grocery business in the neighbourhood of Donkey Common. Overtures were made to a tradesman at 104, Rylance Street, Ardwick, for the purchase of his business, which position, in the opinion of the Board, would be a most suitable one for the establishment of a branch, having such a large and growing population around it. The purchase was accomplished, and the price for the fixtures and goodwill was agreed upon at £210, the remaining stock to be taken over at valuation. Various alterations were carried out, and the business opened on November 11th with a large influx of new members. The business rapidly grew to such an extent that other structural alterations had subsequently to be carried out.

PRESIDENT.

The Quarterly Meeting held on November 22nd received the resignation of Mr. Cuss, who had been President of the Society since its formation, being compelled to take this action consequent upon the loss of business he had sustained through his retention of that office. His resignation was accepted with feelings of extreme regret, especially seeing it was necessitated through interference with his private business. The meeting, however, tendered him hearty thanks for his past services and valuable advice.

W. BROOKS,
President.

PRESENT AUDITORS.

Mr. George E. Stott, our late respected President, was unanimously elected to fill the vacancy.

Mr. Stott was born in Brunswick Street, C.-on-M., and received his education at the Cavendish Day School. At the age of thirteen he entered the employment of Mr. James Andrew, letterpress printer (with whom he served an apprenticeship of seven years as a compositor), remaining with that gentleman altogether a period of fifteen years.

In 1885 he entered the service of Mr. J. Butterworth (afterwards the Market Street Press), being subsequently appointed foreman, a position he held for some years, leaving there to go to the firm of Messrs. H. Rawson and Co., with whom he remained until his death.   He was a staunch teetotaler, and for many years took an active part in the work of the Onward Temperance Society, in Fairfield Street, Ardwick.   He was respectively Secretary and President of that Society, in addition to advocating, indoor and outdoor, the cause of total abstinence.   Like every other sensible man, he got married.   This important event took place in 1885.

In politics he was an ardent Liberal, and was for many years connected with the Beswick Liberal Club, of which he was for a time the Honorary Secretary.   He was respectively the Honorary Secretary and the Chairman of the Beswick Liberal Council, and took an active part in nearly every election in the district for many years.   He had the honour of taking the chair at meetings addressed by W. Mather, Esq., J.P., the late Professor Munro, Alderman Crosfield, &c.

As to religious matters, he was connected with the Ancoats Congregational Church, in which he took a warm interest. He had been a deacon for some years, treasurer of the Sunday School, and was one of the secretaries of the P.S.A. since its inauguration six years ago.   He was essentially a Beswick man.   He was connected with many movements having for their object the amelioration of the condition of the working classes, and was a member of the late Beswick Relief Committee formed to relieve the distress caused by the dispute in the engineering trade.

E

He was elected a member of the Beswick Co-operative Society's Committee in August, 1894, and was re-elected each succeeding year. On the retirement of Mr. Cuss from the position of Chairman in November, 1897, he was unanimously elected to fill the position for the remainder of Mr. Cuss's term, and was subsequently (February, 1898) re-elected for a term of twelve months, which office he held continuously until death relieved him of his duties.

It is rather a coincidence that two gentlemen elected to the highest office in the Society should have been in one profession, for Mr. Stott, like his predecessor, was a printer.

It is with sincere regret that mention has to be made of the great loss this Society sustained on January 21st, 1907, in the death of our esteemed President. It is felt especially keen by myself, in so far that Mr. Stott was one of the Sub-Committee to whom the draft copy of this history was read, and that he did not live to see in print a work in which he was so interested.

Mr. M. Roberts was elected on the Committee in the position vacant by the election of Mr. Stott as President. Mr. Axon, one of the Auditors, also tendered his resignation at this meeting, owing to his removal from the neighbourhood, and his position was filled by the late Secretary, Mr. J. Ashhurst. The remuneration of the Auditors was also increased from £2 to £3 per quarter.

Early Closing.

The Committee, advocates of early closing and supporters of the assistants' half-holiday, decided to close all our establishments, commencing January 8th next, on Saturday evenings at eight o'clock instead of nine o'clock. It perhaps takes our customers a short time to get used to an alteration like this, but when the arrangement is for the betterment of a section of humanity one should take kindly to it and school themselves into it. It is outrageous the hours some shop assistants have to work, and those who employ them appear to have no conscience except for self. It is with pride that the Co-operative employé can speak of his employers in this respect, especially so in the case of this Society.

CHECK SYSTEM.

Consequent upon many losses sustained by members who, having lost their check sheets, necessarily lost their dividend, it was considered advisable to so change the system that, though members may lose their checks, they should not lose their dividend. The system in operation was known as the Eccles, or Gum Sheet, and it was to the interest of members to take care of their checks by gumming them on a sheet and sending it in at quarter end to rank for dividend. The new check system suggested, known as the Climax, patented by Mr. A. Clare, of Farnworth, was credited with being the most accurate and up-to-date system to be used in connection with the many intricacies of a Co-operative Society. The essential part of the system is that members should see their correct membership numbers are stated on the checks given at the time of purchase. The rest is easy, for the duplicates are sent in to the office, compared with the cash, and then posted to each member's account, according to the numbers on the checks. The total for the quarter is then entered on a receipt, and given to the member in exchange for the pass book. If the total does not agree with the member's addition the checks should be returned to the office without delay, as, by wrong numbers on checks, dividend passes to other members. This system was commenced with a new quarter on April 21st, 1898, and, though some difficulty was experienced at the outset, it is now working satisfactorily. The system entails a lot of clerical labour, but this is compensated by the fact that members have ceased to lose their dividends by loss of checks. You will, therefore, observe it is most essential that correct numbers should be given to ensure a correct result.

OUR ANNUAL SOCIAL GATHERING.

I think this is how the affair of November 27th should be described, rather than by the old-fashioned title of "Tea Party." It was far more than a mere tea meeting—it had a good infusion of sociability and more than a suspicion of business in it. And, by the way, I wonder if the members generally have any idea of the amount of work and worry inseparably connected with a gathering of this description: the engaging of artistes, the anxiety about tickets, the uncertainty as to how many to provide for, the selection of a place and the getting ready of the rooms, table fixing and cutting up, and the thousand and one things that go to the making up of a successful social evening. No; I don't believe the average member thinks of these, but the Committee do, and a lively time I know they have had. Some of them were at St. Mary's Schoolroom, preparing and decorating, very late on Friday last, and on Saturday most of the Committee were in evidence. It was fortunate that so many ladies (the wives of the Committee-men and others) were present, otherwise "cutting up" must have been in arrears, and they well deserved a hearty vote of thanks. Before leaving this part of the subject I would like to observe that I think the Committee should not be under the necessity of slaving away at night, fixing tables and carrying forms; the Society is now well able to pay for such work to be done.

It was later than I had intended when I arrived at the Schoolroom on Saturday afternoon, and I was surprised and delighted to find so much had been done and the preparations well advanced. The rooms looked splendid. Row after row of tables, covered with snow-white cloths, lines of plates (one for each person), semi-circles of cups and saucers (kindly lent by the Wholesale Society), and all the "etceteras" that go to complete a well-set tea table. The room was tastefully decorated, the platform was a mass of foliage, and the tables were prettily set with plants, &c.

On the doors being opened the rooms were quickly filled, and at 5-30 every seat was occupied by what proved to be a very hungry gathering. But this had been anticipated. Piles of sandwiches, meat and ham, were placed before them; meat pies, sweet breads, biscuits, buns, tarts, and so on, were all in evidence. The tea was hot and good, and so, after grace had been sung, everyone set to work with a will to reduce the pile in front, but all to no purpose; as quickly as cups were emptied the ladies refilled them, as the plates were cleared the gentlemen replaced them with a further supply. The provisions held out and all were well satisfied, a large amount of stuff being left on the tables.

I must add that, although warnings had been given that the number was limited, and that no one should come without a ticket, yet they came, and accommodation was found for them in another room, and, so far as eating and drinking goes, they fared equally with the others. Now that the Society numbers over 1,500 members, and is "still growing," it might be advisable to have two gatherings—one in Bradford and one, as usual, in Beswick.

The rooms having been cleared, the company was readmitted for the address and concert. The chair was occupied by G. E. Stott, Esq., the new President of the Society, supported by the General Committee, Auditors, and Secretary. Invitations had been sent to all neighbouring Societies, and delegates were present from Manchester Equitable, Droylsden, Pendleton, Failsworth, &c., &c., also Mr. Frank Hardern, J.P., from Oldham.

The Chairman explained why he held that position. Mr. Cuss had resigned the position of President of the Society at the last Quarterly Meeting for reasons connected with his private business, as explained by him to the meeting. He (Mr. Stott) was elected President, and thus found himself quite unexpectedly called on to preside at this annual gathering. He expressed doubts as to his ability to fulfil the duties of the position satisfactorily, but promised to do his best, relying at the same time on the assistance of his colleagues and the hearty support of the members generally. He then briefly referred to the progress the Society had made and was still making—an increase of over 500 members in twelve months and a proportionate increase in sales; the recent opening of another branch, and the fact that five establishments had been opened in five years, and this by a small Society. He pointed out how loyal the Society was to the Wholesale Society, and said it was desirable that all members should be equally loyal to their Store. He strongly deprecated the practice of running all over the town for what appeared to be bargains. If members would but do *all* their trade at their own shops there would be no more successful Society in this part of the kingdom. (Loud cheers.)

Mr. Hardern then addressed the meeting, and said it gave him great pleasure to address such a gathering. He had lived a long time in Oldham, but was really a Beswick man. He could look back over thirty years and remember the neighbourhood as green fields. " I have been looking round to-night," continued Mr. Hardern, "and find the district well grown, and I am glad to find that a good Store has grown with it. Your Chairman calls it 'a little Society'—it is not such a little one. I find it one of the most successful in the kingdom, and it will have its effect on other Societies—its example should be catching. Then there is a social side to the Stores question, and this must be of great benefit to the members—it's nice to see father, mother, and children all together at these gatherings. I like only to go where I could take even my youngest daughter." Referring to the tea which had just finished and the concert about to commence, Mr. Hardern said : " Your programme reminds me of a man who used to get drunk in a very funny way ; the man would first have a whisky, then ale, then whisky, then another ale. One day I asked him why he did so, and his answer was, 'If I drunk ale all night I should be full before I was drunk, and if I drunk whisky only I should be drunk before I was full, but by mixing them I get full and drunk about same time.' (Loud laughter.) So," continued Mr. Hardern, "to-night you will be both pleased and enlightened. I commend your loyalty to the Wholesale, and I ask you to continue united, and your progress is assured. There is, indeed, no telling what you may become. (Loud cheering as Mr. Hardern resumed his seat)

Mr. Allan Schofield (a member of the Committee) proposed, and Mr. Thomas Chadwick (also a Committee-man) seconded, a vote of thanks to Mr. Hardern for his addrees.

Mr. Johnston (Manchester Equitable), in a few well-chosen remarks, supported the proposal. He said the Stores strove only for what they considered their own, and did not try to injure anyone. He said that although his Society had 12,000 members, and there was also Beswick and other Societies at work, yet a stranger coming into Manchester would not see much evidence of the fact, and it was evident that Co-operation has yet much to do, both in trading and in improving the lot of the workers.

The vote of thanks was passed most heartily, and Mr. Hardern briefly acknowledged it.

The concert was then proceeded with, the whole being given by Mr. Harry Oswald's Concert Party, consisting of Miss E. Baldwin (soprano), Miss A. Richardson (contralto), Mr. Fred Crowe (tenor), Mr. Noah Johnson (bass), Mr. Harry Oswald (humorist), Mr. Tom Taylor, a blind young man (instrumentalist), with Madame A. Hudson as solo pianist and accompanist. The programme was long and varied; encores became so frequent that they had to be declined, as they were taking up too much time. In the case of Mr. Johnson the audience would take no refusal, so, after "Simon the Cellarer," he gave "Jack's the Boy," and Mr. Oswald, after "A Village Entertainment," had to give "The Idler." The whole was thoroughly enjoyed by a large and enthusiastic audience, some of whom must have had a "stitch in the side" after hearing Mr. Oswald's "I've got the Ooperzootic." I should add that so touched were the audience with the appearance and performance of Mr. Tom Taylor (who is quite blind) that a special collection was taken up for his benefit, and a goodly sum was the result.

The usual votes of thanks to the Chairman, Committee, and helpers brought a pleasant evening to a close.

November, 1897.

The above report gives one a glimpse of our annual gatherings even at so early a stage in the Society's career.

1898.

On April 4th the Society became agents of the Co-operative Insurance Society for the purpose of conducting business on behalf of our members, and also to obtain the benefit of commission upon our own insurances; the Society at a later date became members of the Insurance Society by taking up shares.

———

Prior to the ordinary business of the Quarterly Meeting held on May 23rd the following resolution was unanimously adopted :—

That this meeting has heard with profound regret of the death of the Right Hon. W. E. Gladstone, and desires to place on record its sense of the great and unparalleled services rendered by him to this country for so many years. This meeting also desires to tender to Mrs. Gladstone and family their sympathy with them in their deep affliction.

The following acknowledgment was received :—

HAWARDEN CASTLE, *June 11th, 1898.*

DEAR SIR,

On behalf of my mother and the family I beg to thank the Beswick Co-operative Society for their very kind message of sympathy.

I remain,

Very faithfully yours,

A. E. WORSWICK, Esq.   (Signed) H. J. GLADSTONE.

The largest sum ever taken for depreciation purposes at any particular Quarterly Meeting was £950 allocated to various buildings, fixtures, &c., at the meeting just referred to. This decision has tended to relieve many succeeding quarters of expense. at the same time forming a good asset. It was also decided at this same meeting to pay a differential rate of dividend on the sales in the butchering department. However, after a few quarters' trial it proved a retrograde step and a continually decreasing turnover, so that it was subsequently decided to revert back to the original arrangement and pay full dividend on the sales. It was considered, and rightly so, that it was unjust to penalise those members who dealt loyally with the Society, because it did not affect in the slightest degree those who did not purchase from the butchering department.

NEW WAREHOUSE, &c.

With the business growing rapidly, and accommodation for storage, stabling, &c., limited, the Committee were compelled to seek additional land on which to erect suitable premises. Land being at such premium in Beswick, one can imagine the difficulties the Committee had to contend with, and at this period there was not much available land to secure. With the intention of purchasing a site in Albert Street, on which to erect a warehouse, bakery, coal yard, and stables, a Special Meeting of the members was called, and on June 21st details of the plot were laid before the meeting. It contained about 1,530 square yards, and the price named at about £1,000 freehold. It was thought that the plot could be purchased at a considerable reduction, and power to close was vested in the Committee. But, upon the solicitor's investigation of the deeds, other unforeseen difficulties arose and the negotiations were discontinued. The Committee laid another offer before the members on November 7th, who gave power to the Committee to purchase any plot of land found suitable, without having the necessity to call a Special Meeting to ratify the purchase, such requirements greatly interfering with the process of negotiations. The meeting also decided to appoint four gentlemen from their general body to work in conjunction with four members of the Board as a Land Purchase Committee

This Committee consisted of Messrs. G. E. Stott, W. Brooks, E. Taylor, J. W. Coles, A. Cuss, J. Ashhurst, W. Kayton, and A. E. Smith. Mr. Kayton, however, did not act on the Committee, owing to extreme pressure of business. The Committee pursued their investigations exhaustively, and many plots were considered, good, bad, and indifferent. Eventually on December 1st they decided to purchase a plot situate in Rowsley Street, having an area of about 2,060 square yards, from Messrs. S. Kershaw and Sons, agents for Sir Oswald Mosley, Bart., for the sum of £600—equal to 5d. per yard on a 22½ years' purchase for net building land. This Committee completed their purchase by having the seal of the Society attached to the deeds conveying the land to the Society from Sir Oswald Mosley, Bart., on January 9th, 1899.

Overtures were also made by this Committee to the owner of an adjacent triangular plot, which, if secured, would make the above plot into a splendid acquisition and almost square ; at the same time the Society would gain many extra yards that would otherwise be required for a passage along the boundary of Beswick and Bradford. But not until April 18th, 1899, was the land question settled with the owner of the adjoining plot, who, being desirous of purchasing our plot for the erection of buildings planned out and receiving an emphatic refusal, saw the futility of holding out, knowing that by the erection of our premises he would be hemmed in with his building, if erected, reopened negotiations, and the purchase was completed for £200, permission being given by the members in Quarterly Meeting on May 15th. Thus the combination constituted the cheapest purchase of land, either before or since, for a most desirable plot, and almost square, which would supply the space for most of the Society's requirements for new Central premises.

In the consideration of how best to cover this land the Committee held rather ambitious views, and the drawing out of plans was entrusted to Messrs. F. Smith, Walsingham, and Smith. It was intended to erect a commodious warehouse, bakery, stables, coal yard, and cart shed on one half, and grocery, drapery, boots, butchering, furnishing, and tailoring shops, offices, boardrooms, public hall (to seat 1,000 persons),

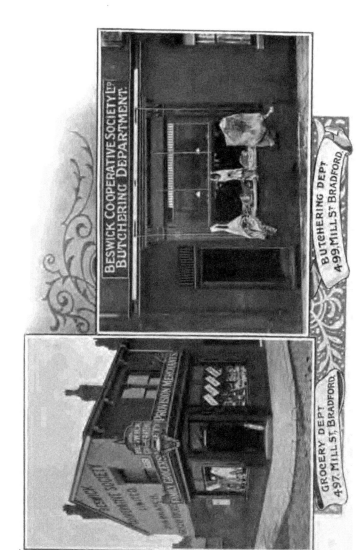

BESWICK COOPERATIVE SOCIETY LTD
BUTCHERING DEPARTMENT.

BUTCHERING DEPT.
4-99, MILL ST, BRADFORD.

GROCERY DEPT.
4-97, MILL ST, BRADFORD.

library, reading-rooms, ante-rooms, and a house for the manager or caretaker on the other half. The working plans were to be so arranged that procedure could be taken with the first half at once, being urgently required, without interference with the other portion of the plot.

MILL STREET BRANCH.

In view of opening a grocery branch in the vicinity of Mill Street, Openshaw end, a member of the Committee had been making inquiries. Reporting his success on July 4th, he considered that the shop, 497, Mill Street, Bradford (Openshaw end), at present occupied, would be a very desirable position, it being on offer. The fixtures and goodwill were purchased for the sum of £10, and a lease of tenancy arranged with the landlady at a rental of £26 per annum. Various alterations were made to adapt the premises to our requirements, and the business was opened on September 8th. It has since justified its existence by its turnover, which so increased that further alterations had to be made, and subsequently other branches opened to relieve the congestion—a most encouraging feature in a Co-operative Society.

CHILDREN'S LURRY TRIP.

August 13th was the date of the first lurry trip for the children of the members, arranged for their enjoyment in the country. Twenty-six lurries took the children to Reddish Vale, where refreshments and amusements were provided. The subsequent years' trips grew to such abnormal dimensions that it was reluctantly abandoned, the last occasion requiring the provision of over forty-five lurries, and in its stead a field is secured in Clayton for a great Field Day, and which has since taken place year by year with complete success.

The following is a letter from a member eulogising our Field Day, which was received in August, 1903, and inserted in the " Wheatsheaf " :—

To the Local Editor.

SIR,—As an interested member and willing helper on the occasion of our Children's Field Day, on July 4th, I, in common with many other members, desire to place on record our high appreciation of the efforts and

labour of the Committee in such a gigantic undertaking. Never was there
such a day for a children's picnic, as all who were present know, and, as
those who were absent hardly need telling, everything was full of sunshine
and a brilliant success.   It was noted that the workers vied with each
other to make the occasion a most enjoyable one for the young Co-
operators assembled.   On all hands special praise was being meted out
for the excellency of the refreshment catering.   With regard to the races
on the field, marked ability was shown by those responsible for the
handicapping of the competitors.   Being at the finishing end of the
courses, I was able to judge by the many expressions of the onlookers at
the results.   The useful prizes awarded were much appreciated by the
winners, and well envied by the unsuccessful ones.   Here, again, great
praise was accorded for the very excellent and judicious selection.

In conclusion, the best thanks of the members are due to the Co-
operative Wholesale employés who so generously presented the special
prizes competed for by the first winners of the races.

Yours respectfully,

An Appreciative Member.

Boundary, not Amalgamation.

Our neighbours were greatly concerned over the rapid
extension of the Society's business and the progress we were
making.   The Committee materially assisted by their assiduous propaganda work—distributing " Wheatsheafs," balance
sheets, and other literature, and making a house-to-house
canvass.   It is not everyone who would undertake to do this
kind of solicitation for the furtherance of any cause.   Yet
our Committee had no scruples, but took bundles of literature
under their arms, and invited the public to seriously consider
about joining our Society after reading through the facts
given them.   Although the weather was not always propitious
yet it did not deter their visits, which brought about very good
results.   This propaganda work showed great interest on the
part of our Committee for the welfare of the Society, and
should, therefore, be greatly encouraged.

The Manchester and Salford Society wrote deprecating the
Committee's action in arranging to open a branch at 497, Mill
Street, and desired to hold a conference on the question at an
early date.   They were met on August 11th, when the whole
question was gone into, giving the reasons for the existence of
this Society.   They desired that we should seriously consider
the outlining of some boundary to limit our operations, as
they were anxious to arrive at some definite understanding.

They were asked, however, to suggest a boundary they considered reasonable for our deliberations. Instead of which, we presumed, they placed the question in the hands of the Co-operative Union, to whom we disclaimed giving any authority for the preparation of a boundary. The Union replied, in support of their action, that two years ago the question of a boundary line was under consideration, and that our Society thought nothing could be done until some boundary line was suggested, hence the preparation of one by them. They further intimated that one had been prepared, and that the Boundaries Sub-Committee would like a joint conference of the Committees of the Beswick and Manchester and Salford Societies with them on neutral ground with a neutral Chairman. It was decided, seeing that the question of a boundary line had not emanated from us, and we had not asked them to form any boundary line, we do not see our way to enter into any conference on the question.

Penny Bank.

On October 3rd the Committee thought the time had arrived when a Small Savings Bank might be beneficially included in the Society's business, for the purpose of encouraging thrift amongst the children of our members and others. To do this, however, it was necessary that the rules of the Society should be amended, there being no provision in the same to receive loans on deposit. The rules were so amended at the Quarterly Meeting of members on November 28th, and advantage was taken of the opportunity to amend the rule relating to interest on share capital, making the interest at 5 per cent on sums up to £75, and 2½ per cent over £75, by which means it was intended to debar purely investing members. The rules were registered, and the Penny Bank was commenced on March 6th, 1899, and has now successfully grown to over 5,000 depositors.

An Attack.

Some person or persons evidently had spleen against the Society, for it came to the knowledge of the Committee that slanderous statements were being circulated which would have a damaging effect upon the Society.   We know there are numerous enemies to our movement, who do not trouble to consider that our object is a good one—the amelioration of the conditions of the people, and to raise the tone of the social side of life. They have only a selfish aim, and, therefore, an axe to grind.   The Committee caused the following legal notice to be printed, circulated, and posted on the walls, the effect of which announcement was an abrupt termination of these statements, and confidence was again restored in the minds of our members, albeit the Society was in a sound financial position.

WARNING.

Whereas it has come to the knowledge of the above Society, having its Registered Offices at 70, Ashton New Road, Beswick, Manchester, that some person or persons have recently been circulating statements which tend to damage the credit and standing of the Society.

Notice is hereby given that the Committee of the said Society will give a reward of £50 to any person or persons giving such information to the undersigned as will lead to the conviction of the offenders.

Dated this 12th day of October, 1898.

ROWCLIFFE & CO.,
30, Cross Street, Manchester,
Solicitors to the said Society.

CONSTITUTION OF THE COMMITTEE.

The members gave permission to the Committee on November 28th to increase their constitution to nine members, to deal with the largely increasing business. Mr. Schofield was appointed to the additional position.

CHAPTER V.

—

1899—Boundary.

THIS question of a boundary was ever before the notice of this Committee without seeming to get one step nearer the solution, the Manchester and Salford Society assiduously agitating without offering any palliative. A deputation from the Co-operative Union (Messrs. Percival and Whitehead) waited upon the Committee, stating that their Committee had prepared a boundary line, which they believed would form a reasonable basis for argument upon the question of overlapping between Beswick and the Manchester and Salford Societies. They desired to know if the Committee would meet the Manchester and Salford Society and the Boundaries Sub-Committee on neutral ground with a neutral Chairman to discuss the question. To this the Committee acquiesced, and nominated Pendleton Society's premises as the place of meeting, with Mr. Hemingway as Chairman, the date to be fixed for February 24th.

The conference took place, at which the very existence of the Beswick Society was challenged, and, after the reasons were given for its establishment, an expression was given that the Beswick Society had come, and come to stay, and must, therefore, be recognised by the movement. The boundary, as drawn up by the Union, was all in favour of the Manchester and Salford Society, and simply tied the Society down to its present very limited area, namely, a line as the crow may fly (not irregular) from point to point where our various shops are located. This, of course, coincided with the views of the Manchester and Salford Society, though they considered it a great concession on their part to agree to. But Beswick Society's opinion had also to be considered, who strongly protested against the suggested boundary, which allowed of no expansion to a growing Society, and gave the opinion that unless it was made considerably more elastic no satisfactory conclusions would be arrived at. The result of this conference was given to the members in Quarterly Meeting on February 27th, who appealed for the information, and it was resolved, " That the Committee do not entertain further the boundary line question as suggested between the Co-operative Union and the Manchester and Salford Society."

At the meeting of the Committee on March 3rd a requisition signed by over 150 members was received, requesting the Committee to call a Special Meeting of the members for March 10th, for the consideration of the following resolutions, which were carried at the meeting held :—

That the Committee ignore the boundary line question with the Co-operative Union and the Manchester and Salford, passed at the Quarterly Meeting on February 27th, be rescinded, and

That the Committee complete the negotiations on the boundary question, and report to a general meeting for final decision.

The Co-operative Union, after the above decision, desired permission to send a deputation to our next Quarterly Meeting, with a view to securing some amicable arrangement on the boundary question.   This permission was given, but to facilitate matters, and to try to obtain an early settlement of the vexed question, it was decided to call a Special Meeting for April 11th for the following business :—

To receive a deputation from the Co-operative Union, and to consider a suggestion as to agreeing to a boundary line between this Society and the Manchester and Salford Equitable Society, and to adopt such resolution or resolutions thereon as the meeting may deem expedient.

with this injunction on the notice calling the meeting—

The effect of a boundary line, if adopted, will be that the operations of this Society will be confined to its present limited area, and that no new branches outside this area can be opened.   It will thus be seen that this question is one of the utmost importance to every member of the Society, and we trust that there will be a large attendance at the meeting on April 11th.

The meeting was held, and the deputation received.   They spoke at some length upon the question of a boundary between this Society and the Manchester and Salford Society, and asked the meeting to give power to the Committee to settle the question with the Co-operative Union of a boundary line which would be amicable to all parties concerned.   A resolution was, however, moved and carried by a large majority, " That we do

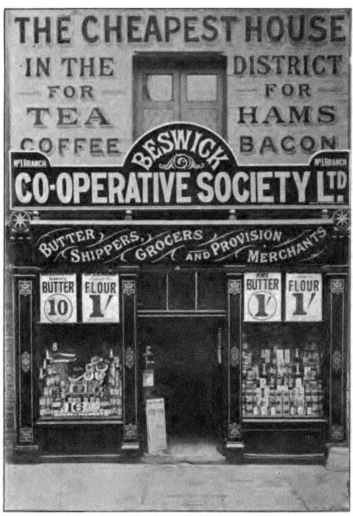

No. 2 BRANCH, 150, BUTLER STREET, ANCOATS.

F

not carry forward the negotiations for a boundary line or enter-tain the question further." Messrs. Watson, Percival, and Whitehead were accorded a vote of thanks for their presence.

A letter was, however, received on May 1st from the Manchester and Salford Society stating that they had heard that the whole of the negotiations during the last few months to amicably arrange matters between the two Societies had ended (so far as Beswick was concerned) so hopelessly, and contrary to the most elementary principles of Co-operation. To this the following reply was sent :—

*The Committee, Manchester and Salford
Equitable Co-operative Society.*   *May 4th, 1899.*

GENTLEMEN,

   I beg to acknowledge receipt of yours dated April 25th. Although the nature of it calls for no reply, yet it seems as if your Committee were of opinion that all the time and labour of the conferences had been in vain, and the Committee are desirous, if at all possible, to remove this impression. It is quite true that our members have refused to sanction any boundary line between the two Societies, and would not agree to any suggestion as to a working arrangement, yet the Committee are anxious to remove any misunderstanding as to their intentions.

   It has been stated that the Society was about to open out branches at Ardwick, Openshaw, Longsight, the Polygon, &c. With the exception of Ardwick, there is no likelihood and certainly no intention of doing anything of the kind, at any rate, for a long time to come, and if the Committee do accede to the request made to them to open a branch in Ardwick, care will be taken to select a position which will avoid, as much as possible, any competition.

   Though the Committee are aware that you would have preferred to have a boundary line fixed, yet, under the circumstances, they trust that this note may remove some of the impressions that undoubtedly exist with regard to the operations of this Society.

                         Yours truly,
                         Pro Committee,
                              A. E. WORSWICK, *Secretary.*

On February 27th the Auditors received an advance in their remuneration from £3 to £4 per quarter, owing to the largely increased duties attendant.

No. 1. BRANCH TRANSFERRED.

It was decided on May 29th to transfer the business of No. 1 Branch from 149, Mill Street, Ancoats, to more commodious premises at 150, Butler Street, Ancoats.   The change was for the better, the premises being cleaner, more sanitary, and better adapted for the business.   It has proved such by the largely-increased trade, being now double that at Mill Street.   The new premises were opened on June 8th.

VISIT TO IRLAM.

The members made a visit of inspection to the C.W.S. Works at Irlam on September 23rd, and each member of the party received a parcel of samples for the purpose of having a test of the goods manufactured.   The party was taken through the Works by guides, who explained the whole process of soap making.   It proved a very interesting and instructive visit, especially the manufacture of glycerine, which, although it looks so pure and nice, the environment of its production was rather obnoxious to the sense of smell.   After seeing the ingredients that go together in the making of soap, &c., one can highly recommend the members to use C.W.S. Soaps, &c., as being value for money, and of the highest quality with full weight.

EDITOR'S SALARY.

The Editor of the Society's portion of the "Wheatsheaf," having to spend much time over his editorial work in addition to his duties as Committee-man, made application for some recognition of his services.   His attention was drawn to Rule 4, which made it impossible for him to hold two paid offices under the Society, and he would have to relinquish his seat on the Committee if paid for his services as Editor.   It was thereupon decided that Messrs. Stott, Brooks, Chadwick, Clark, and Schofield should form a Sub-Committee to amend the rules, and the following new rules were submitted, along with other amendments, to a Special Meeting of the members, on November 27th, and received their approval :—

NEW RULE.—SERVANTS AND OTHERS WHO ARE NOT TO BE OFFICERS.

Any person carrying on a similar business, on his own account, to the Society shall not be eligible for any office or service, neither shall any servant of this Society serve any office in the Committee of Management or be an Auditor.

No. 6 BRANCH, 2, ELLIOTT STREET, BRADFORD.

68, 70, 72, ASHTON NEW ROAD, BESWICK.

ADDITION TO RULE 4.

No person shall be eligible as a member of the Committee of Management or any Special Committee, or for any other office, who does not hold at least one fully paid-up share in the funds of the Society, and is a purchasing member.

No person shall be eligible for a Committee-man who has not been a member of the Society for twelve months, or eligible for the office of President who has not been a member of the Committee for twelve months.

NEW RULE.—REMUNERATION OF OFFICERS.

The ordinary quarterly business meetings shall from time to time determine the remuneration of the President, Committee-men, or any other member for their services as they think fit.

NEW RULE.—CASES OF DISTRESS OR REMOVAL.

The Committee may from time to time repay to any member in distress, or for satisfactory cause shown, the sum then credited upon any transferable shares held by him or her (less a deduction of 1s., which shall be appropriated to the reduction of fixed stock), and upon a resolution of the Committee to that effect such share or shares shall be extinguished.

It was not until after the registration of the above amendments that the Editor received any remuneration, but the salary of £4 per annum voted on February 26th, 1900, was made retrospective.

NEW EXTENSIONS.

Double events are interesting affairs, and such was the occasion on October 26th, by the opening of two additional places of business. The boot department was separated from the drapery department at 235, Ashton New Road, and transferred to 68, Ashton New Road, on the expiration of the tenancy of Mr. Wainwright, whose Manageress was taken into our employ. The other shop was a grocery branch at 2, Elliott Street, Bradford, the goodwill and fixtures having been purchased from the then present tenant. The two shops have proved a capital convenience to the members, especially the grocery shop, which at the present time is doing a large turnover.

PLANS—NEW PREMISES.

Messrs. Smith, Walsingham, and Smith, Architects, submitted three sketches for selection of buildings proposed to be erected on the land in Rowsley Street and Key West

Street, and one was chosen by the Committee which was on view at the Quarterly Meeting held on August 28th. An estimate of the cost was drawn out, and would total about £13,700, this amount being exclusive of the machinery, &c., required. When submitted to the Quarterly Meeting on November 27th the members resolved to give power to the Committee to proceed with the erection of the proposed buildings. It was, however, decided by the Committee to only proceed at first with the erection of the most urgent buildings, viz., those of the warehouse, bakery, and stables, costing about £6,000, the remaining portion of the land to remain unoccupied until such time as the present proposal was satisfactorily completed. Final plans were afterwards completed and deposited with the Corporation for approval, and during the lapse of the few months they were in their possession the drainage was proceeded with.

ARDWICK BRANCH.

Notwithstanding the amount of time and thought occupied over such an important matter as the above, another grocery branch was secured at 37, Ogden Street, Ardwick, and was opened for business on December 22nd. The members in this district had sent in a requisition, signed by a large number, asking the Committee to open a branch near Union Street for their convenience, as our nearest branch was at a considerable distance. The establishment proved a great boon to our Ardwick friends, and has since been highly appreciated, judging by the volume of trade done.

BOUNDARY.

The boundary question was continuously before the Board, especially so when opening new branches. A protest was lodged by the neighbouring Society with the Committee for having opened a branch in Elliott Street, which was considered their ground, and that such an action was against the interests of Co-operation. It is an open question whether the ground was theirs or not, and one may ask : Of what use is any area to anyone if insufficiently worked ? It must be

GENERAL
COMMITTEE.

W. ALCOCK.

T. CHADWICK.

J.W. COLES.

G. KILBOURNE.

J. NUTTALL.

T. PHILLIPS.

G

A. SCHOFIELD.

W. TAPLIN.

E. TAYLOR.

W. WALKER.

in the interest of Co-operation for the local Society to take a district in hand where no provision is made.   The branch, however, has proved its necessity for establishment by the fact that its turnover is over £100 per week.

Consequent upon our progression the Committee received an invitation from the Manchester and Salford Society to appoint three delegates to attend a conference of the Societies in the Manchester district on the question of over-lapping by the Beswick Society, on Saturday, January 13th, 1900.   Messrs. Stott, Brooks, and Clark were appointed to attend and watch the interests of our Society.   It was thought desirable and advisable to state our case to the many Societies who would be represented at this conference by circular, so that they might have an opportunity of discussing our true position before the conference, and so be prepared in the discussion that would transpire.

1900.
BOUNDARY.

Our delegates attending the above conference gave a full report of the overlapping question as submitted, and the result of the deliberations was to the effect that the two Societies concerned, the Manchester and Salford and Beswick, should meet the Co-operative Union to arrange matters amicably, the conference feeling they could do nothing in the matter.   However, a new feature developed upon the question, showing that we were not the only Society who had cause for complaint against the existing state of affairs and the allocation of the various workable areas of Manchester and district.   The Pendleton Society approached us to see if we were agreeable to appoint two delegates to attend a joint conference on the boundary question to rearrange the working area of the Manchester Societies, the same to be convened by the Co-operative Union.   We agreed to the proposal, and appointed Messrs. Stott and Clark as our delegates.   The conference was held on March 2nd, and in the report of same to the Committee it was mentioned that the Manchester and Salford Society had refused to take part in any conference unless called by the Co-operative Union ; also intimating that they would not consider any boundary question until such had been settled between themselves and the Beswick Society. The Chairman, Mr. Hemingway, stated that the question under consideration would probably take a matter of twelve months to settle, and that the presence of the delegates at the next conference bound those Societies represented to abide by the decisions arrived at by the joint conference. Our delegates had clearly pointed out to the meeting that we could not possibly accept a boundary such as had been drawn up by the Union, and that in this proposed conference we should not accept a boundary that did not allow us a reasonable growth ; and that we should have to place any suggested boundary before our members to decide. The Chairman, in reply, said that our members had better give permission to the Committee to settle this matter, as it was a question of urgency. All the Societies in the Manchester district of the Co-operative Union were invited to take part in this joint conference ; and the Committee agreed that if they took part in the conference they would pledge themselves to abide by the decision of the joint conference.

At a meeting on March 19th a deputation from the Co-operative Union, consisting of Messrs. Percival, Fairbrother, Hardern, and Whitehead, waited upon the Committee and asked them to guarantee not to open business out of the prescribed area, as drawn up by the Co-operative Union for the last conference between ourselves and the Manchester and Salford Society, during the deliberations of the proposed joint conference of the Manchester Societies on the boundary question, to which the Committee expressed their willingness to agree.

PREMATURE DIVIDENDS.

On January 29th the Committee decided, owing to our district being an ever-changing one by the removal of residents through their business avocations, and consequently many of our members are compelled to withdraw their membership, to allow, in cases of this kind, the payment of a 2s. dividend on purchases that have been made since the last declaration of dividend, and which cannot be left to rank for the next

No. 8 BRANCH, 37, ASHTON OLD ROAD, OPENSHAW.

dividend, this amount being fixed obviously to meet the contingency of a reduced dividend next declared and so place the Society within a satisfactory margin. This arrangement should meet with the approval of those who are compelled to withdraw from the Society, as otherwise they would not be members at the time of the disposal of the profits, and, therefore, not entitled to participate in same.

SHOP HOURS.

The Committee on March 5th again reduced the shop hours to seven o'clock Monday and Tuesday, and half-past seven o'clock Saturday evenings, and remained thus for several years. Members soon got used to the reduced hours, and would as soon adapt themselves to a further reduction if it was thought desirable. This reduction placed the employés under a distinct advantage over those in private trade, and they fully appreciated the action of the Committee.

To safeguard any possibility of a loss by the butchering Manager when making his purchases of cattle at the live market, a deposit of £100 was made with Parr's Bank, who, upon a small commission, paid the accounts of our purchases, afterwards rendering us a statement. This is a capital arrangement, saving our buyer both time and anxiety, for it saved him the necessity to carry cash for his purchases, strictly cash being the terms in the market.

LEGAL ADVISERS.

On March 12th our legal affairs were placed in the hands of Messrs. F. O. S. Leak and Pratt, John Dalton Street, and their advice has been eminently reliable on matters of law. They have been the means of saving the Society from many pitfalls to be found in litigation, and thus much expense. They still act in the capacity of our legal advisers.

NEW BRANCH.

On April 9th we received an offer of a grocery shop at 37, Ashton Old Road, Openshaw, from the tenant of same, and, being considered a most desirable position for a grocery branch of the Society, was secured by the purchase of goodwill and fixtures. The house portion was occupied by a separate tenant, which brought in revenue towards the rent. A tenancy was arranged with the landlord, and the branch was opened for business on May 24th.

PROPERTY, MILL STREET, BRADFORD.

On April 23rd the Committee received, from the owner of the property, Mill Street, Bradford, the option of purchase of our present shop and three houses adjoining, the price being £800. The revenue was £80 per annum, and the chief rent £10. Messrs. Stott, Brooks, Schofield, and our Architect made an inspection of the property, and strongly recommended the purchase at the price named, deeming it a desirable acquisition. The members, at their meeting on May 28th gave permission to the Committee to purchase the property at the price mentioned. The conveyance was completed on August 13th, and the deeds handed over to us, so that the property, 497, 499, 501, and 503, Mill Street, Bradford, became part of the assets of the Society.

FEES.

At the Quarterly Meeting held on May 28th, in consequence of the Editor of our portion of the " Wheatsheaf " being paid for his services, and additionally as a Committee-man, it was resolved : " That it is inexpedient, and also contrary to Co-operative principles, that one member of the Committee should occupy two positions of profit under the Beswick Co-operative Society, and that any member holding two paid offices be requested to resign one of them forthwith." The Editor tendered his resignation of that office, and the vacancy was filled by Mr. James Rowbottom.

This meeting also increased the remuneration of the Committee for general meetings to 2s. per meeting.

BOUNDARY.

As a result of opening the branch at 37, Ashton Old Road, a deputation from the neighbouring Society waited upon the

Committee, stating that they would like us to discontinue this competition between them and us. They had tried to secure the shop referred to, but had heard we had taken it. The Chairman, however, gave the deputation to understand that we had promised the Co-operative Union not to extend our business beyond the suggested boundary they had drawn up pending the result of the joint conference on the boundary question, and that this shop comes within that suggested area.

After this deputation, and on September 10th, the Committee wrote the Co-operative Union pointing out that our hands were tied from extending our business pending a joint conference, and requesting information of when a conference is to be held on the boundary question, as they were desirous of being relieved of their promise not to open business out of the suggested area. A reply was received that after various important matters occupying the attention of the Boundaries Sub-Committee were completed the conference would have first consideration. The Committee, however, replied that they wished to be relieved of their promise to the Co-operative Union, although they had no present intention of opening business out of the suggested area, but that our members in meeting assembled gave definite instructions to them not to proceed further with the question of a boundary line between ourselves and the Manchester and Salford Society.

A conference was called for October 2nd, at Balloon Street, to consider the question of overlapping, and Messrs. Stott and Chadwick were appointed to attend. The decision arrived at was that forms should be issued by the Co-operative Union for the purpose of obtaining information of Societies overlapping, and that these Societies should submit their cases to a board of arbitration to decide their various positions, and in case of Societies who would not agree to this mode of procedure stringent measures should be taken, with expulsion from the Union, subject, of course, to these proposals being adopted.

A further conference was held on December 22nd at Balloon Street, " To discuss the present state of affairs existing in the Manchester district in regard to overlapping, and to endeavour, if possible, to arrive at an amicable settlement for the fixing of new boundaries between the Societies concerned." Messrs. Stott and Kilbourne attended, and reported that during the discussion a delegate had stated that the Beswick Society had become established, and that they would have to recognise them as a Society in their considerations.   Mr. Stott had stated that we were in favour of a boundary line, but that the Committee had received definite instructions not to consider a boundary line between ourselves and the Manchester and Salford Society.   Several delegates pointed out that if boundary lines were adopted the van delivery outside of areas should be abolished.   The following resolution was adopted :—

That in the opinion of this conference the district should be divided into areas, to be agreed upon by the Co-operative Union, and the Societies in such defined areas should at once take steps to meet their neighbours with a view to formulating boundary lines, and where these already exist to ratify or extend.   In case of points of difference arising, the Societies should give an undertaking, in writing, signed by both Societies, agreeing to abide by the decision of the Boundaries Sub-Committee, and the allocation of unworked areas to be left in the hands of the Committee.

NEW BAKERY.

The plans of the new bakery, warehouse, &c., were approved by the Corporation on April 23rd, and tenders for the erection of the buildings were invited, Messrs. Chapman and Hollinworth, of Patricroft, being successful in their tender of £4,790. The contract was signed, and operations commenced later on. With a view of securing the best ovens on the market for the bakery, the Committee made a number of visits to various bakeries, some even at midnight, and saw many different makers' ovens working, also machinery.   They were unanimously of opinion that the ovens of Messrs. Werner, Pfleiderer, and Perkins were the most satisfactory, and placed with them an order for two single-decker drawplate ovens.   Other machinery was also ordered, such as flour mixer, hoists, and gas engine.   The new premises occupied a large amount of the Committee's time and labour in the elevation and the fittings required.

DOUGH DIVIDER  MIXER

OVENS.

Another difficulty, however, had to be met, viz., the ancient lights of adjoining cottage property, the owner claiming compensation for the obstruction of light to his cottages by the erection of our high buildings. The matter was eventually settled by the payment of compensation in settlement of all claims for past or future ancient rights of light.

1901.

Opening Progress Bakery.

It was thought possible to have the formal opening of the new warehouse, bakery, and stables on February 2nd, but owing to the death of Her Majesty Queen Victoria, and the funeral taking place on that date, it was postponed to a week later, viz., February 9th. This was a red-letter day with Beswick Society by the opening of long-looked-for premises, which were of a magnitude never before in our possession. The neighbourhood was alive with people in anticipation of the ceremony. There was a procession of decorated vehicles round the district, and much advertising was done announcing the opening, &c.

The honour of performing the opening ceremony was justly conferred upon the President, Mr. Stott, after which the premises were thrown open for inspection, and a free concert held in the large bakery flour room was well patronised. There was also a large business done in the sale of 1s. parcels of C.W.S. goods. The following is a report of the event, taken from the *Co-operative News :*—

How the Society commenced the Bread Trade.

No small portion of the *News* has of late been occupied with reports of jubilees and openings of bakeries. Both are important landmarks in a Co-operative history. A Society must be well established before it can venture to erect a bakery, and fifty years of storm and sunshine have to pass ere a jubilee comes round. Beswick Co-operators celebrated the first of these events on Saturday. Whether their Society will attain the dignity of a jubilee, no one can tell. Sufficient is it to say that indications point that way. The affair should have taken place the previous Saturday, but was postponed on account of the Queen's funeral. The rain, which hovered about all day, happily kept off ; otherwise, the procession which had been arranged would have suffered. This consisted of a band, a wagonette for the use of the Committee, two lurries, on which were

H

displayed C.W.S. goods, and three or four vehicles of the Society, including its first bread van. The horses were gaily decked with ribbons. The event caused quite a stir in the district, a good number of people following the procession to the bakery. One street in the route deserves to be called Co-operative Street, seeing that every householder is a member of the Store.

AT THE BAKERY.

A temporary platform had been erected in front of the bakery, on which gathered a number of officials of the Society. Round about stood a large crowd of members and friends. Mr. Brooks opened the proceedings. The building, he said, belonged to the working men and women who formed the Beswick Society. It was a splendid and sub-stantial testimony of what could be done by Co-operation. He proceeded to explain in detail how the Society was conducted, and said he wished that the Co-operative system was better understood in Beswick than what it was at the present time. Some people thought that dividend was the all of Co-operators. But this was not so. The Beswick Society was a large supporter of the Bradford Nurses' Institution, and during the late lock-out it contributed generously to the men's funds. The Society had been a boon to many householders in that district, and he claimed that they had carried out what Mr. Hardern said at the Liverpool Congress about Co-operation and the poor. They had found, on a house-to-house canvass, that some persons could not raise eighteen-pence to become members, and the shopmen were instructed to receive that sum in small contributions. In this way they were carrying out one of the chief planks of Co-operation—that was, going to the very poor. Mr. Smith (Architect) spoke a few words, expressing a hope that the Society would go on and prosper.

SKETCH OF THE SOCIETY.

Mr. Stott was the next speaker. He said that he considered it a great honour to be the President of a large body of working men and women to the number of over 3,000. He hoped the step they were then taking was one that would redound to the prosperity of every inhabitant in that neighbourhood. It was nine years since a few gentlemen expressed a need for a Co-operative Society at Beswick, and June, 1892, saw its establishment. All was not plain sailing, but the pioneers stuck to their guns, and ultimately achieved success. At the end of the first year the members numbered 147, the sales amounted to £3,583, the dividend to £124, and the share capital to £456. They commenced business with one establishment, but soon found that insufficient. A branch was opened at Mill Street, and they had that branch still, though it had been removed a little. Instead of the one shop of nine years ago, the Society had now eight grocery stores and numerous other shops for the transaction of its business. The number of members for the quarter ended January last was 3,265, which was very creditable after nine years' work. The share capital at that period amounted to £10,813. The sales for the quarter mentioned were £15,818, which represented a business of £60,000 a year. This was a big increase on the £3,583 for the first year. They had a penny bank, and the depositors numbered 1,630, with £1,280 to their credit. The Beswick Society had done what some Societies had not done, it had gone

WAREHOUSE, KEY WEST STREET, BESWICK.

into the poorer districts. The reason for that bakery was the large trade and membership and the need for more accommodation. They would now be able to produce bread under the best conditions. He then asked not only for greater loyalty, but for some propaganda work. Concluding, he hoped that the bakery would mark a new era in the history of the Beswick Society, that they would continue to go ahead, and that they would bring many to share in the benefits of Co-operation, which aimed at the uplifting of the working men and women of this country. (Applause.) He then read a telegram conveying the best wishes of Mr. Peter Ryder (director), who was away on business of the Wholesale Society.

Mr. Cuss (first member and first President) was the succeeding speaker. After giving an interesting account of the commencement of the Society, he proposed a vote of thanks to Mr. Brooks. This was seconded by Mr. Lord (Wholesale Society).

Mr. Smith then presented a gold key to Mr. Stott as a memento of the Society's position after nine years' hard work. The key bore the following inscription :—" Presented to George Edward Stott, Esq. (President of the Beswick Co-operative Society), on the opening of the new bakery, &c., February 9th, 1901.''

Mr. Stott then opened the premises for the purpose of carrying on the business of the Beswick Society. A large number of persons afterwards made what was probably their first tour through a bakery. A concert in the evening brought the memorable day to a close.

The New Premises.

The bakery, said to be the finest in the north of England for its size, is situated on land of the Society at the corner of Rowsley Street and Key West Street, Ashton New Road, Beswick. The buildings also comprise warehouse, stables, sheds, &c. The bakery is on the most modern and sanitary design, and consists of a bakehouse 30ft. by 30ft. clear of the ovens, lined with glazed bricks, and well lighted on three sides. This room is fitted with two of Werner, Pfleiderer, and Perkins' drawplate ovens, and with space for a third. A cooling platform is provided outside the bakery. Over the bakery, and separated by a fireproof floor, is the mixing-room, 45ft. by 30ft., containing the gas engine, kneading machine, and other appliances, and over this again the storeroom, with the sifting machinery. The warehouse, consisting of five floors, is in the same block, and is fitted with cage and whip hoist (by Higginbottom and Mannock), Manager's office, covered loading way, and every appliance for the receipt and despatch of goods. The stabling consists of three stables of four stalls each, and with loose box, harness-room, and provender store, constructed on the most approved sanitary lines. The vehicle shed, 60ft. by 28ft., covers a considerable portion of the yard, and is roofed with glass. The contractors for the premises were Messrs. Chapman and Hollinworth (Eccles), and the architects Messrs. Smith, Walsingham, and Smith (Manchester). The total cost is over £7,000. The buildings do not occupy all the land, and on the vacant portion it is intended to erect offices, public hall, committee-rooms, shops, and workrooms.

CHAPTER VI.

BRANCH BUTCHERING.

It was thought advisable to open out branches in different districts for the purpose of supplying our members with beef, mutton, &c., and, with this object in view, one of the Society's houses in Mill Street, Bradford, adjoining the grocery shop, was converted into a butcher's shop, and opened for business on February 15th. This served the wants of a very large neighbourhood in the Openshaw district, and on April 30th another butcher's shop was opened, next door to our grocery department in Ogden Street, for the convenience of our Ardwick friends. Unfortunately, however, the business at the latter shop so declined, through a variety of circumstances, that it was found absolutely necessary to close it up at the end of our tenancy.

On April 22nd the Society received notice from the Corporation to provide more yard space and other convenience to our property at Parker Street, and to do this it was necessary to demolish the adjoining cottage, for which we received a weekly rent. This was done, and the only reimbursement the Society got for the demolition of a remunerative cottage was a nominal £15, though, of course, we had some consolation in the compensating ventilation and better convenience than hitherto.

EMPLOYEES' CONFERENCE.

An important conference between the Committee and employés was held on April 30th, at which some very good advice and admonition was addressed to the employés by several members of the Board. The advantages enjoyed by our employés over those employed in private trade are incalculable, and it is only to be expected that they reciprocate the desire of the Committee by serving them to the best of their ability. The Chairman, Mr. Stott, pointed out that the number of members was increasing week by week, but the Committee did not consider that the trade was increasing proportionately.   The Committee were determined that, whatever orders were issued by them to the employés, they must be carried out, and the Branch Managers were expected to report any deviation from those orders.   The Committee's desire was that every customer should be treated with the utmost courtesy, and to make no distinction between poor and richer members.   He said :—

It is of the utmost importance that our shops and warehouses should be kept in a high state of cleanliness, as most of the articles retailed were foodstuffs, and essential to avoid deterioration of our high standard of quality.   It was also important to have the shops opened for business punctually in a morning ; there are some delinquents in this respect, and it may possibly be through their fault that some children are made late for school.

Special attention was drawn to the Food and Drugs Act and the weighing of bread served over the counter. Employés must not neglect to serve goods in the prescribed wrappers, or to supply the deficiency of weight in bread as required by the Act.   The employés should also take particular care over the making out of customers' checks.   It was essential that correct numbers be stated thereon, to facilitate the work in the office.   Much work arose at the time of balancing in consequence of wrong numbers.

It was hoped that the employés would take note of these words of advice, and endeavour to remedy what evils existed for the success and well-being of the Society.

At the Quarterly Meeting held on May 20th the salary of the Auditors was again increased to £5. 10s. per quarter. The following important motion by Mr. T. Phillips was also adopted unanimously :—

(a) Contractors tendering for or executing work under the Beswick Co-operative Society must, if practicable, be employers of labour in the district, and observing the hours and conditions of labour now recognised by the local organised bodies, and be subject to such alterations as may occur in the various trades, no tender to be accepted from any firm who prohibit their workpeople from joining organised bodies.   Any contractor from an outside district whose tender may be accepted shall be required to conform to the rates and conditions of such district; but in regard to any work actually done in this district he must conform to the rates and hours of labour observed in this district. (*b*) Should the Committee have reasonable grounds for believing that the above conditions are not being complied with, the contractor shall be called upon to produce his books to the Manager or Secretary for inspection, showing the names of, wages paid to, and the hours observed by all those employed by him. (*c*) The contractor shall not assign or under-let the contract, or any part of it, or sub-contract, except with the consent of the Committee, and upon such conditions as they may think fit; but if the tenderer at the time of tendering states his desire to sub-let any portions of the work not usually done by him, the Committee will agree to do so with an approved person, the principal contractor being responsible to the Committee for the work being done under the same conditions as if done by himself; and should the contractor or agent give or offer any gratuity to any officer of the Society the Society shall be at liberty to determine the contract. Compliance with this standing order shall be the essence of every contract, and non-compliance therewith, after due notice to the contractor, shall entitle the members of the Society absolutely to determine the contract.

RAILWAY EXCURSION.

On July 20th a railway excursion was arranged for the members to Smithy Bridge, for Hollingworth Lake, and, although the train left Beswick Station early in the afternoon, it was very poorly patronised, only about 200 people travelling. The failure to reach the guaranteed number made it a very expensive experiment for the Society, and very little encouragement in the arrangements of future events of this kind.

The Committee, in August, were of the opinion that the trade of the Society was at a standstill, having up to this period experienced nothing but progression; and, although the general trade in our district and surroundings was one of depression, they decided to make some investigations to find out the cause of our non-progress. Messrs. Stott, Brooks, Kilbourne, and Walker were appointed a Sub-Committee to look into the prices of goods, removals, and non-purchasing members. In their report on October 15th they stated, having visited some 130 members in various districts, they found that it was entirely due to the bad trade in our district and the number of removals caused thereby. Those they had seen had spoken highly of our system, the civility and attention of our servants ; so, therefore, we could rest assured there was nothing wrong with the internal workings of the Society, but rather due to the reduced purchasing capacity of the members.

No. 9 BRANCH, 118, HILLKIRK STREET, ARDWICK.

PRESENT CENTRAL EXTENSION.

The Society's property, 72, Ashton New Road, becoming vacant in October, was taken over for the Society's own business, and the question was : What can it be best utilised for ?   It was thought desirable at first to so alter the shop and the upper rooms of this and No. 70 to make a drapery establishment, but on production of the cost of same the suggestion was abandoned.   Instead, it was fitted up to serve as a useful extension of the present grocery, by adding a provision department, making an entrance internally from one to the other.   The result has been very satisfactory in the greater facilities thus afforded for dealing with the large trade at these premises.

BOUNDARY.

Reverting back to the question which appears to turn up very consistently—the boundary—the Committee, with a view to thoroughly studying the development of the question, appointed Messrs. Stott and Kilbourne to attend a conference on overlapping at Bolton on January 5th.   Intimation was also received from the Co-operative Union that the Manchester district had been divided into areas on the boundary question, and that we had been allocated to No. 1 area, and the first meeting to consider same would be held on January 30th.   Messrs. Kilbourne and Taylor attended, but two Societies in the Manchester district were unrepresented. It was suggested at this meeting that the Manchester and Salford and Beswick Societies should settle their differences between themselves.   Messrs. Stott and Clark were appointed delegates to the Co-operative Congress held at Middlesbrough, as the question of overlapping was to be raised, but in their report it was stated that this question, of particular interest to this Society, was dropped altogether.   It had not, however, been dropped altogether, for we were again approached by the Co-operative Union on June 24th as to whether we had yet considered a boundary suitable for our Society which we would submit to them, and whether we would be agreeable to receive a deputation from them upon the question.   A reply was sent stating that it was our intention to meet the Committee of the Droylsden Society with a view to arriving at some amicable arrangement regarding boundaries ; but that, in regard to Manchester and Salford Society, our hands were tied, the members distinctly declining to allow us to proceed further, and certainly not while the van delivery continued. In these circumstances we did not deem it advisable to receive the deputation. The Co-operative Union wrote again, on September 23rd, that they were anxious to draw up the necessary agreements between Societies if amicable arrangements had been arrived at.

Droylsden Society.

Our Committee met the Committee of the Droylsden Society on October 22nd, at which meeting it was agreed that our Society, in conjunction with them, should recognise a boundary that had been arranged suitably to both parties, thus arriving at an amicable settlement with at least one of our neighbours.

1902.
Hillkirk Street Branch

The Committee in August purchased the goodwill and fixtures from the tenant of 118, Hillkirk Street, Ardwick, and after a tenancy was arranged with the landlord, and the internal structure so altered as to meet the requirements of our business, the shop was opened on January 9th. The trade done at this shop since opening has justified its establishment.

Coal Business.

The commencing of the coal business occupied much of the attention of the Committee, and, being determined to enter what appeared to be—by the number engaged in the trade—a most lucrative business, they set about purchasing horseflesh and rolling stock in October. A circular was also issued to the members, stating that we were about to undertake the coal business ourselves, and desired to learn the

DRAPERY AND TAILORING DEPARTMENTS, 138-140, ASHTON NEW ROAD, BESWICK.

extent of their support, so that we could better arrange to meet the demand.   The response was about 50 tons weekly in the aggregate.   This result was somewhat encouraging, and it was decided to commence as early as possible.   The arrangement with the local dealer was terminated and a Coal Manager engaged, who started the business with the new quarter on January 14th.   It has since proved an undoubted acquisition to the operations of the Society. The trade grew rapidly, and in October it had reached an output of 100 tons weekly, since when it has considerably increased to an average of at least 150 tons per week.   In consequence of the growing trade many horses and vehicles have been purchased to thoroughly deal with it.   The employés in this department are given every encouragement to push the trade, both in hours of labour and wages, and we think the coal supplied is of the best procurable.   The Society owns railway rolling stock to the extent of twenty wagons, five of which have recently been added, and their purchase has saved us a large amount of money that would have been charged for hire.   In fact, fifteen have practically been paid for by the assumed charges.   An office was purchased conveniently situated at the railway coal depôt, Rowsley Street, from a local dealer who was removing his business, and the ground rent arranged with the Lancashire and Yorkshire Railway Company.   In summing up we can say, without fear of contradiction, that this business is the most remunerative to the Society.

REMOVAL OF DRAPERY DEPARTMENT.

In November of last year the Committee had to consider the question of the tenancy of the drapery department, 235, Ashton New Road, which ended at Christmas.   They received an offer from the proprietor of the drapery business at 138–140, Ashton New Road, and, being two very good, large shops, were favourably impressed with them.   Eventually they agreed to purchase the goodwill and fixtures.

The landlord accepted us as tenants on a lease ; and, after various alterations were carried out in the manner peculiar to all premises rented by us before any business can be done in them, the premises were opened for business on March 14th, the goods having been removed in the meantime from the other address.   The tailoring department was considerably extended now that we had such large premises, and the business result was shown separately in the balance sheet at a later date.

ELECTION OF COMMITTEE.

At the Quarterly Meeting held on February 24th Mr. Phillips made several suggestions relative to the manner of election of Committees, and, after some discussion, he moved :

> That four scrutineers be appointed, whose duties shall be to see that every member in the room receives a ballot paper on which shall be printed the names of the candidates, two scrutineers to hand out the ballot papers.   Members having marked the ballot papers, the other two scrutineers to collect them ; the votes to be then counted and the result declared.

The resolution carried, and it was desirable, seeing that previously the voting papers had been given out to members upon entering the meeting-room, and did not act satisfactorily.

CARTERS' MAY DAY.

The Committee introduced what was an innovation amongst the carters of the Society—an annual inspection of the horses on May 1st.   Prizes were given to those carters whose horses showed best attention, both for cleanliness and decoration.   This was an encouragement to the carters, and each one did his best to outshine the others.   The Committee have continued this arrangement to the present time.

VISIT TO CRUMPSALL WORKS.

A visit was arranged for the members to the C.W.S. Crumpsall Biscuit Works, by kind permission of the Directors, on Saturday, August 30th.   It was a most enjoyable outing, and about 250 persons participated.   Making the journey by char-a-bancs and stage coaches, the party, on arrival, were conducted through the Works by several guides, who explained the different rooms and processes, which was both interesting and instructive. When leaving the Works each person was presented with a splendid box of samples of C.W.S. manufacture. The Blackley Co-operative Society kindly undertook to provide a good tea in their central premises, after which the drive was continued through the new acquisition of the City Corporation—Heaton Park—permission being kindly extended to us. It was, without doubt, a successful and profitable afternoon's outing, and fully appreciated.

CO-OPERATIVE BOYCOTT.

In October the Co-operative movement was attacked by the Private Traders' Association, and to combat this unwise action on the part of the traders the Co-operative Union formed a Defence Fund to meet the tactics of a boycott. Societies were invited to contribute a guarantee in proportion to their status, with the ultimate result of a fund of £100,000, the Co-operative Wholesale Society having guaranteed £50,000. The agitation was commenced in St. Helens, and carried to Wigan and other places, the official organ of their movement being the *Tradesman and Shopkeeper*, which endeavoured to nurture the agitation. The newspaper, however, received a severe check to its career in 1906, as a result of an unwarranted attack on our Plymouth friends The proprietors had to appear at the Law Courts, along with the printers, on a charge of libel, and suffered very heavy damages. After this verdict was given the agitation, having lost prestige with a great many traders, seemed to die a natural death, and in its stead an innovation installed at the place of its birth to endeavour to counteract the progress of the Co-operative movement by the traders of St. Helens forming an association to pay a dividend to customers. How it succeeds I am not in a position to state.

The boycott adopted drastic measures when in operation, going to the extremity of approaching employers of labour and demanding the dismissal of employés who were connected with any Co-operative Society, with success in some cases, though in others the employers could not see the force of their arguments in liberty-loving England. Others, of course, severed their connection with the movement to retain their

J

livelihood.   It was a rather mean spirit to exhibit, and was not
of a truth met in the same spirit in our movement, our object
being defence, not defiance.   The Co-operative movement
has done more for the amelioration of the conditions of the
working classes and their social life than will ever emanate
from such an association of the kind referred to.   However,
the result of their methods simply provided the means of a
splendid advertisement of the good work Co-operative
Societies were doing, and opened the eyes of the people to
such an extent that membership and sales were swelling
considerably.

With the object of this Society taking its proper share in
this defence, and contributing our quota towards bringing
about an early termination of the agitation, a requisition
signed by twenty members was received on October 20th,
asking the Committee to call a special meeting of the members
to discuss the following resolution :—" That the Beswick
Co-operative Society shall contribute to the Co-operative
Union Defence Fund to fight the unfair boycott directed
against our movement by the Private Traders' Association,"
with the intimation that it was their intention to support
such contributions as might be necessary to cover our share
of the expenses incurred in the campaign, such sum not to
exceed in the aggregate £100.   The meeting was held on
November 3rd, the Committee supporting the resolution to
guarantee the sum of £100 to the fund, which was carried.
We have only been called upon to pay 5 per cent of the
guarantee money, so that it proves the uselessness of
initiating such a boycott.

BRANCH SUGGESTED.

In November the Committee came across a site in Bank
Lane, Clayton, that was considered would be suitable for the
establishment of a branch for the convenience of our Stuart
Street members, who desired such convenience, there being
none within reasonable distance.   As it was situated on the
boundary between ourselves and the Droylsden Society, it
was decided to ask the Droylsden Committee to receive a
deputation with a view to obtaining their permission to open
a branch on the site mentioned.   Messrs. Stott, Brooks, and

Kilbourne comprised the deputation, who were duly received, and as a result of that conference the following decision was arrived at :—The Committee of the Droylsden Society, after carefully considering the proposal, regretted being compelled to arrive at a decision unfavourable to us. They stated that previous to the agreement being drawn up between the two Societies they had opened negotiations for a site in Bank Lane for the establishment of a branch, and which were still open. They suggested that, several sites being vacant in Stuart Street, one might be secured that would be suitable to us, and under these circumstances they thought it was only fair that the agreement should be maintained.

At the time of writing no branch has yet been established by either Society in this growing district, and though several attempts have been made by our Committee to secure a suitable site in Stuart Street, it is hoped that we may yet be successful, for there is no doubt that we continue to lose trade through the want of a branch.

Shop Hours.

On November 17th the Committee decided to extend the hours of the drapery, boots, and tailoring departments on Saturday evenings to 9-30, but subsequently reduced to 8-30, for the purpose of making a convenience for members to purchase goods required for the week end which had been overlooked during the week. So that the employés concerned should not work any additional hours the extra time was taken off other days in the week.

Non-Members' Dividend.

At the Quarterly Meeting held on November 24th, Mr. Sheldon, a member, moved the following resolution :—

That on and after the 25th day of November, 1902, a dividend of 1s. in the £ be allowed on all purchases by non-members, and that a check be given to all non-members for the amount of their purchases, and endorsed "non-member;" such checks to be exchangeable any time at the Society's Office, during office hours, for cash in amounts of not less than £2 in purchases, and that a notice be placed in a conspicuous position in each of the Society's places of business drawing the attention of non-members to the fact that a dividend is allowed on their trade.

The merits and demerits of the motion were fully discussed, and it was eventually agreed to.   The new arrangement, with the exception that the dividend was increased to 1s. 8d. per £ on amounts of 10s. upwards, was fully advertised by hand-bills and other form of announcement, but the payment of non-members' dividends has not yet reached anything like substantial proportions.   It may be accounted for by those non-members, seeing that these slight advantages can be much improved by being members, joining the Society, thereby increasing the membership roll and reducing the non-members' dividend.   The system commenced with the new quarter on January 13th, 1903.

CHAPTER VII

—

1903

FROM time to time we have been faithfully served by our employés, but unfortunately there have been cases—though happily few—where circumstances have created suspicions of dishonesty, and consequently the Society had to part with those employés. Generally speaking, the Society is very fortunate in the selection of its servants, for they use every ability for the benefit of the Society.

Occasionally, too, the Society's establishments receive a visit from the burglarious fraternity, who, in the hope of finding money, are generally disappointed, and in a fit of spitefulness leave the place in great disorder. There is some satisfaction in knowing that many have been apprehended and received their just deserts. The Committee on one occasion very rightly complimented a constable on his plucky action in apprehending two men who were clearing with sacks our boot department window at Ashton New Road, Beswick.

At the February Quarterly Meeting a fund was formed for the equalisation of dividend on members' purchases with the sum of £100. The fund has now grown to over £1,000. It is a matter of sound finance to adopt funds of this nature to look to in time of necessity, and should be encouraged

A DOUBLE VENTURE.—NEW CENTRAL PREMISES.

Plans of new hall, boardroom, offices, and two shops, to be erected on the land in Rowsley Street, were approved by the Committee on February 20th, and by the Corporation about May. Tenders for the erection in accordance with the quantities issued by our Architects were invited by the Committee, and on July 14th the contract was given to Mr. Robert Carlyle, of Old Trafford, for the sum of £7,594, the work to be finished by May next.

LAND, ASHTON OLD ROAD.

Towards the close of last year an offer of land situate on Ashton Old Road, fronting what was known as Donkey Common, was received by the Committee. It was a most desirable plot for the establishment of good business premises, especially in view of the fact that there were only this and two other plots available for purchase which might soon be secured.

The hands of the Committee were somewhat tied by the erection of new Central premises in Rowsley Street, but, nevertheless, negotiations for the purchase of the land were opened. The area of the plot was some $942\frac{4}{9}$ square yards, with a frontage of $43\frac{2}{3}$ yards; the frontage being paved and sewered, though the side streets were not. The price eventually agreed upon was £1,154. 10s., free from chief. A Special Meeting of the members was held on April 20th to approve the purchase or otherwise, and the Committee were empowered unanimously to complete the purchase on the terms named, subject to the conditions in the contract of sale being satisfactory. The seal of the Society and signatures were affixed to the deeds of conveyance on June 29th.

Mr. W. H. Aldred, Architect, was thereupon instructed to draw up plans for a three-storey building, to include grocery, drapery, boots, tailoring, pork and butchering shops; cellars in the basement; store and showrooms on the first floor; and workrooms on top floor. Tenders were invited for the erection of a building of this kind, and on July 14th the contract was given to Mr. Edward Jackson, of Openshaw, for the sum of £7,200, the work to be completed in about eight months; so, therefore, on July 14th the Society gave out contracts for the erection of buildings to the extent of about £15,000—a rather large undertaking.

MORE LAND.

Another vacant plot of land, situate in Vincent Street and Croft Street, Higher Openshaw, was offered to the Committee in June and favourably considered. The plot had a frontage of $134\frac{1}{2}$ feet, and a depth of $50\frac{1}{2}$ feet, or 750 net building square yards; the total area being about 1,407 square yards. The streets surrounding required paving and sewering, and the price asked was £275, on a chief of £13 per annum. The Committee decided to call a Special Meeting of the members for July 6th to ratify the purchase of the land, as in their opinion it would be a decided acquisition for the establishment of a branch to cater for a neighbourhood that was growing so rapidly. At the same time it would provide a convenience for those members who were compelled to make their purchases at Mill Street, and thereby help materially to reduce the present congestion and thus avoid expensive alterations that would of necessity have to be carried out to cope with it. The members upon meeting unanimously gave permission to the Committee to complete the purchase of the land in question. The Committee explained that it was their intention, upon acquiring the land, to erect one grocery shop at the earliest possible opportunity, which would not be, however, before the present large buildings in course of erection were completed ; and leave the remaining land vacant until such time that they could see their way to either add other departments or house property as may be decided.

The seal and signature of the Society were affixed to the deeds conveying the land to the Society on August 31st.

On May 11th it was resolved to forward the following petition to the Right Hon. A. J. Balfour, M.P. :—

Showeth—That your petitioners are deeply interested in the Bill now before your honourable House which has for its object the "Prevention of Corruption in Trade," as they believe that the measure, if passed into law, will effectually prevent the corrupt practices which are known to exist in trade and commerce.

The measure was introduced by the Attorney-General. Mr. Balfour acknowledged receipt of this petition, and stated that he would take an early opportunity of presenting it to the House. A Bill similar to this became law in January, 1907.

ADDITIONAL COMMITTEE-MAN.

On May 25th the Committee sought power from the members in Quarterly Meeting to increase the constitution of their Board by an additional member, in support of which they drew the attention of the meeting to the increasing business of the Society, and consequently the work thus entailed. Power was granted, and it was decided to elect the additional member by nomination at the next Quarterly Meeting, thus increasing the number on the Board to eleven members, inclusive of President. Mr. T. Phillips was elected to the additional vacancy.

BOUNDARY.

On July 14th the Committee were again written by the Manchester and Salford Society asking if they would receive a deputation from them on the question of a boundary line. A reply was sent to the effect that we could not see the utility of an interview on this question, seeing that we had on several occasions met them without arriving at any decision or any likelihood of a result. There had been no fresh developments, but if they desired to see us on a particular boundary and would submit it, the Committee would give it their careful consideration.

Thus ended practically all intercourse on the question of a boundary line, for we have not since been approached upon the question, and I am happy to say that we have to all intents and purposes become most friendly with our neighbours, and work amicably together in the furtherance of the Co-operative cause.

BONUS TEA.

The Committee, on September 29th, as a result of a conference of Managers at the C.W.S. on the question of tea sales, considered the desirability of introducing the system of bonus tea, with a view to somewhat increasing our sales and combat the private traders' present-giving system, and at the same time assist our sales in other departments. The Manager was instructed to make inquiries from other Societies who had adopted the bonus tea system of its influence upon their trade. He visited several Societies and reported that they all spoke highly of the system in vogue, and of its advantage in the sales of tea. St. Helens did a very large business in it, and Burnley had increased their trade to ten times its weight of tea since introduction. Due consideration was given to the question and to the facts submitted, and although our percentage of tea sales was good compared with other Societies, yet it fell considerably below the national consumption figures, being only 12lb. out of a possible 30lb. In these circumstances it was considered advisable to introduce the system to our members with the sole object of increasing our tea sales and retaining trade in other departments that was taken elsewhere. It was thereupon resolved: "That we adopt the bonus tea system at some future date to be fixed, as, in our opinion, it will be both beneficial to the members and materially increase our sales in tea." The Manager, Secretary, and three members of the Committee visited several Societies near Manchester to study the manner of conducting the system. It was eventually decided to commence the system on February 22nd, 1904, fixing the prices of bonus tea to include a bonus check value 10d. per lb., which check could be spent in any department except grocery, butchering, and coal. It was also decided to make it widely known that the members were paying 10d. extra per lb. for their tea to obtain these bonus coupons. There is nothing misleading or underhand in this system, whereas private dealers refrain from telling their customers the value of their coupons, simply stating that so many coupons are required for any particular article. I am afraid there is a great deal of bias in the movement against this system, which has been taken up by so many Societies, and against the packing of such a commodity by the C.W.S. Sentiment may be responsible for a great deal of bias, but this quality to a great extent has to be sunk in matters of business ; and where there is nothing but openness in the dealings, how can we be charged with violating our principles ? I do not seek to vindicate our attitude upon this question, but simply to comment upon it from a broad standpoint, and one of business.

At the Quarterly Meeting held on November 23rd it was resolved to take up twenty-five £1 shares in the North Wales Quarries Limited. It was so invested to encourage a new Co-operative venture, formed for the purpose of finding labour for many men unemployed in Wales caused through a strike for better conditions. The company has suffered considerably for want of capital, but a better response is being experienced, and it will eventually, it is hoped, prove a successful venture.

AMENDED RULES.

The same Quarterly Meeting was made special for the purpose of amending rules as follows :—

ADMISSION, REFUSAL, OR EXPULSION OF MEMBERS.

2.—No person shall be admitted as a member of this Society except by the Committee of Management. Every person admitted shall have his name, place of abode, and occupation or profession entered in a book provided for that purpose, and pay an entrance fee of sixpence, which shall cover the cost of pass book and rules. He shall, on election, take at least one transferable share.

It was a progressive step to take in the reduction of the entrance fee to 6d., as the nominal fee, charged to cover cost of books, should not deter even the poorest person from joining and participating in the benefits to be derived by being a member of the Society. The reduction has tended to increase the membership roll.

Rule 20 was proposed to be altered, but was referred back for further amendment, and when submitted to a Special Meeting on December 21st it was passed in its entirety.

INTEREST ON SHARES.

20.—Each member shall receive quarterly out of the surplus receipts of the Society, after providing for the expenses thereof in each quarter, interest not exceeding 5 per cent per annum upon paid-up shares up to £75, provided such member's purchases shall amount to £2 per quarter, and on shares over £75 interest not exceeding 3½ per cent per annum that may have been standing to his or her credit during the preceding quarter, conditionally upon such member's purchases amounting to £5 per quarter. Members purchasing less than the amount required by this rule shall not be paid more than 2½ per cent per annum.

The object of this alteration was to increase the capital of the Society, owing to extensive building operations and other requirements. The increased interest over £75 would induce many members who were not simple investors to leave in their capital instead of withdrawing above that sum, and also induce deposits. There was, however, a condition attached : that of purchases to the extent of £5 per quarter, but this was no great hardship, though it showed that the Society does not encourage members who simply use the Society for investment. It is always much more desirable to pay the interest to members on their capital than to pay it to bankers for an overdraft, and this was the intention of the Committee when the alteration was recommended.

The amended rules were included in a complete form of amendment, and when the certificate of registration was received from the Registrar copies were issued to the members in February, 1904.

1904.

This year was a very busy one indeed for the Committee, and one of great importance in the extension and progress of the Society's business. The hands of the Committee were full in the approaching completion of the two new premises, and the work of internal fittings required much time and thought to thoroughly equip them to meet the requirements of the Society's business. Consultations with the architects and contractors were many on various matters, and inspection on others ; and a sigh of relief was heaved when the premises were declared satisfactorily completed. The readers must, however, judge for themselves of the stupendous task in the following pages.

BRITISH COTTON GROWING ASSOCIATION.

At the Quarterly Meeting on February 22nd the members considered the question of making a contribution towards the formation of the British Cotton Growing Association, which association had for its object the acquirement of plantations for the supplying of home demands in cotton, and ultimately become independent of the United States supply. It has been recently experienced how the withholding of supplies by America crippled the staple industry of Lancashire by fluctuating and exorbitant prices, consequent upon the gambling of New York and other American Exchanges. The Committee recommended the members to contribute to the object, and they generously voted the sum of £25—a fair proportion compared with the status of the Society. The association, when it became chartered, allotted the amount as shares, but, having been paid out of the balance disposable, these are not included in the Society's assets. The association has justified its existence by the good work it is doing, having secured many plantations in different parts of the world, which will eventually yield cotton to materially assist the requirements of home manufacture. The association, however, requires more capital to develop still further the scope of its operations, and it is to be hoped will meet with the ready response it deserves from those directly concerned in the industry.

ASHTON OLD ROAD NEW PREMISES.

When the contractor, Mr. E. Jackson, gave in May a date when he anticipated handing over the new premises on Ashton Old Road the Committee fixed as the date of the formal opening ceremony June 25th, and to open for business on June 23rd. Arrangements were made for making it a red-letter day in the history of the Society, and such it turned out to be.   A procession of decorated vehicles, and a char-a-banc full of Committee, officials, representatives of neighbouring Societies, together with those responsible for the satisfactory completion of the premises, paraded the district in the vicinity, headed by a brass band.   The attention of the residents was thus called to the important event, and inviting them to become members of the Society by means of literature distributed *en route.*   Mr. W. Brooks, member of the Committee of many years' standing, was unanimously given the honour of performing the opening ceremony, Mr. Stott acting as Chairman of the proceedings.   A concert was held in the evening in the large hall, and, only a nominal admission being charged, was crowded.   A marble tablet, bearing the names of the Committee, officers, architect, and builder, was erected in the large hall by the architect and builder, commemorating the date of opening.   The large hall, by the way, was an afterthought of the Committee when the premises were approaching completion.   The original intention was to fit up the top floor as workrooms, but the dimensions were such that it was considered it would be more remunerative as a public hall, let off for engagements, than workrooms which may not be required for some years to come. This judgment has been realised beyond anticipation, and the hall is a splendid source of revenue, adding to the profits after allowing sufficient to cover the expenses on the outlay.   The

No. 10 BRANCH, 217, 219, 221, and 223, ASHTON OLD ROAD, ARDWICK.

various shops have done good business since opening, showing the necessity for the establishment of these premises for the convenience of members in this district. One hundred and twenty persons were admitted members of the Society at the Committee meeting following the opening ceremony.

Appended is a full report of the proceedings as appeared in the *Co-operative News* :—

IMPOSING CEREMONY ON SATURDAY.

The members of the Beswick Society, at Manchester, have displayed much energy in various directions during the past few years, and the interesting ceremony which was witnessed on Saturday last—the opening of a branch right in the heart of one of Manchester's typical working-class districts—has left a lasting impression on those whose pleasure it was to attend and whose interests are keen in the direction of extending Co-operation among the poor of our large cities. This Beswick Society seems to be unparalleled in its success. The secret of this is not far to seek, for there is no half-heartedness in the policy and aims of the members of the Committee. The mere opening of shops and the declaration of a dividend are altogether inadequate to fill the horizon of the imaginations of those whose one absorbing interest is to make Co-operators—not members only.

THEN AND NOW: SINGULAR DEVELOPMENTS.

It is twelve years ago since the Society was first started, and nine years ago, when Mr. Brooks—who opened the new branch premises on Saturday—was elected on the Committee, the Board of Management had to sit on empty cheese boxes, and every bit of work had to be done free of expense! In 1892, when the Society was registered, there were seven members; to-day the membership reaches over 4,800. The sales for the first quarter were £700, and for the last quarter, ending April 11th, 1904, £25,460, or a yearly trade of over £100,000, while the dividend paid to members last year, at the rate of 2s. 9d. in the £, was £12,943. "To the energy of Mr. Roddis (the manager), the employés, who are second to none, and the criticisms of the members at the Quarterly Meetings, I attribute the cause of all these increases," said Mr. Brooks. "Advice and criticism from the members we always welcome, and when a lady member ventures to speak on the cash accounts, as one did at the last quarterly, we can indeed pride ourselves that another progressive step has been made." To-day this popular Society has as many as ten grocery establishments, and when the new premises in Rowsley Street are completed all will be within a quarter of an hour's walk from the central. It really seems as if the people of Beswick clamoured for Co-operation, for it is not unusual to go through a labyrinth of streets and find Co-operators at every house. And this is, as already stated, right in the heart of a great city. "Clearly something has been done to revolutionise the neighbourhood," said a *News* representative to Mr. Brooks and Mr. Stott (the President) on Saturday. "Yes," they replied, "we have taken the movement to the doors of the people, and in the winter-time we have visited the people in their homes."

Further conversation with Mr. Chadwick (another Committee-man) revealed the news that the entrance fee was now only sixpence, and the shopmen had authority to take this in instalments of 2d. and 3d. a time.

THE SCENE ON SATURDAY.

A corner of Ashton Old Road, Ardwick, where the branch has been erected, was the point of concentration, so far as general curiosity was concerned, on Saturday. A flag hoisted over the new premises, the C.W.S. tobacco factory band, and a great gathering of people helped to make the "show." Bathed in sunshine, the handsome pile of buildings of bright terra-cotta brick had an air of stately dignity in a neighbourhood where everything else looked dull and grey. And the crowd gathered round the platform had a character quite its own. Men and women, some in holiday attire, others in their working clothes, had all come out to wish "God-speed" to the Committee and their new enterprise. It is difficult to do justice to the enthusiasm which prevailed, but the remark of one woman member—who called out, "And the members, too," when Mr. Stott stated that Saturday was a proud day for the Beswick Committee—showed the keen interest which the members generally take in their own Society.

In his opening remarks, Mr. Stott (the President) said that at one time in his life he used to dread coming past the piece of land on which their new shops now stood, and he certainly never dreamt that he would ever become the President of such a progressive little Society as they had in Beswick that day. They were making members at the rate of fifty to sixty weekly; in fact, since the opening of the new shops on Thursday, fifty-eight new members had been enrolled. They bought the best, and sold only the best, at such prices as would allow for the payment of the best wages. (Cheers.) He appealed to the working men—and they were all working men on the platform, although they might have their best clothes on— (laughter)—to help on the Society to still greater achievements. "Why," said Mr. Stott, "I met a man this morning, one who does hard work, who was wearing a pair of Co-operatively-made boots which had only been repaired once after three years' hard wear." (Loud cheers and laughter.)

CO-OPERATION FOR THE POOR.

Mr. Kilbourne (another Committee member) remarked that if the Beswick Society was not one of the largest in Lancashire, it was one of the best. (Cheers.) He compared the opening of the new stores to the launching of a new ship, when no one claims to having made or done any special part, but where each looks upon the whole and thinks of the little he has done. Co-operation was intended for the poor, and no greater evidence of that could be shown than the existence of the Beswick Society, which was pitched right into the midst of the working classes. He begged of the members to invest their savings in the Society, and trust their fellow-men with their money, instead of putting their capital into the hands of others, who used it for their own personal advancement.

At this juncture Mr. Aldred (the architect) presented Mr. Brooks with a silver key, wherewith to open the door. In the course of his address, Mr. Brooks showed what the Society did for the poor by giving to the various hospitals. Their members did not always want all the dividend, for it was no difficulty to get grants and donations passed, and in their wisdom, instead of receiving a 3s. 1d. dividend, they preferred 2s. 9d., the remaining 4d. to go towards depreciation, which, of course, meant that the Society was financially safe and sound.   On £26,000 they had depreciated to the extent of £5,709.   (Loud applause.)

Another speaker was Mr. W. Lander (of the C.W.S.), who gave a stirring address.   He hoped the Beswick Co-operators would not become apathetic on account of their success, but rather the success would be the means of rousing their interest in the Co-operative movement.   Then the steps they were taking that afternoon would not be stumbling blocks. The equal distribution of the wealth of the country would help to make slum life impossible. He pleaded with his listeners to help on the movement which did away with millionaires on the one hand and paupers on the other. Through shopkeeping on their own account they could amass wealth, and with wealth they could become more intelligent, and intelligence would bring unity of interests and hope for the workers towards an easier, a brighter, and better life. (Loud applause.)

THE NEW SHOPS.

After the usual votes of thanks, the people filed into the new drapery, grocery, boots and shoes, tailoring, and butchery shops, the capacity and fittings of which are worthy the greatest merchants.   There were electric lights everywhere, together with goods of C.W.S. manufacture.   The butcher's shop, with its immaculate and pretty decorative tiles, is most ideal, while the cellars, where meats are cooked – and in which the Society does a good trade—are not to be surpassed for cleanliness.   The building itself is three storeys high.   The second floor will be used for showrooms, and on the top is a Co-operative Hall and various ante-rooms.

The latest information is that from the Thursday to the Saturday the sales in the new shops amounted to £229, and as many as eighty-three new members were made.

A LAST IMPRESSION.

There have been many openings of new Co-operative premises perhaps more impressive in splendour, but I do not remember (writes our representative) where everything went more pleasantly.   There was such a ring of sincerity about the whole proceedings, which were most impressive. Not that impressiveness which comes from eloquent speeches, but an inspiriting effect, due to the feeling that everyone was concerned in his fellow-workers' welfare.   Co-operation is a real Aladdin's lamp, and Beswick Co-operators keep their lamps well trimmed. "We intend to keep up our educational work," said Mr. Stott and Mr. Brooks to our representative, as they journeyed to the new central premises, which will be opened in August next.

In the evening a concert took place in the new Hall, when Mr. Stott again presided.

Among others prominent at Saturday's function were noted Mr. Worswick (Secretary of Beswick Society), Mr. J. T. Taylor (Oldham), Messrs. Stansfield and Heyes (Manchester and Salford Society), and delegates from Bolton, Mossley, and other surrounding Societies.

K

CHAPTER VIII.

—

The Auditors had their remuneration increased to £8 per quarter at the Quarterly Meeting held on May 16th, in consideration of their numerous duties being greatly increased. At the same meeting the Chairman announced that the next Quarterly Meeting would be held in the Society's own premises, and invited the members to meet an hour earlier on that occasion to view them. Therefore, this meeting would be the last in the room where all the Quarterly Meetings of the Society had been held since establishment, to which many associations could be attached. The room was becoming too small for the accommodation of the attendance, but it was like parting with an old friend going to other premises.

The Committee had a stupendous task when they advertised for two hallkeepers to look after the two new premises. Whether it was caused by the state of the labour market or the anticipation of easy occupation it is hard to say, but 900 applications were received for the two positions, the qualifications supporting which being various and humorous. The Committee, after taking off their coats for the task, eventually made a selection, from which two capable men were appointed. There is always a good response for vacancies in the Co-operative employ, and very few instances of resigning their appointments, but the response to this advertisement constitutes a record in our Society.

NEW CENTRAL PREMISES.

The Committee decided upon August 13th as the red-letter day for the formal opening of the new Central premises in Rowsley Street, the contractor, Mr. R. Carlyle, having promised to have them ready for handing over early in August. It proved truly a red line in the calendar in the Society's history, for the Committee made elaborate arrangements for a deserving celebration. The procedure was similar to the opening of the Ashton Old Road premises, with equally good results. Mr. George E. Stott, the President, was given

ASSEMBLY HALL

STAIRCASE

REGISTERED OFFICES

the honour of performing the important ceremony of declaring the premises open for business, thus completing his work of 1901, when he declared the bakery and warehouse open, adjacent on the same plot. Mr. T. Chadwick acted as Chairman of the proceedings, and was supported on the platform by the Committee, officials, representatives from neighbouring Societies, Mr. Walsingham, architect, and Mr. Carlyle, contractor. The procession in the district caused much attention to be drawn to the existence of the Society, and great progress has since been the result. The shops have done good business, the public hall has proved itself to be a long-felt want in the neighbourhood by the manner in which it has since been engaged, and the offices and boardrooms have provided a convenience that was very much desired. The officials and clerks are enabled to work with more energy than hitherto, which may be readily understood when considering the fact that previously about eight employés had to work in an ordinary-sized bedroom with little ventilation, and who had to retire on meeting nights to allow the Committee to deliberate on matters of business, under conditions by no means conducive to retaining clear minds.

The order of things is thus changed, and, without doubt, fully appreciated. The employés have plenty of room in which to breathe and to do their work satisfactorily, with plenty of ventilation and proper sanitary accommodation. The boardroom is a comfort to meet in and transact the important business of the Society, and the wonder is how it was previously carried on under such depressing circumstances.

Without further comment a report of the proceedings, which appeared in the *Co-operative News*, is appended of the splendid acquisition to the Society's business assets :—

STRIKING FACTS OF PROGRESS.

The leading features of Beswick Society's new central premises, in the heart of one of Manchester's most populous working-class centres, were shown and described to a *News* representative some six or seven weeks ago. But since then rapid progress has been made, and on Saturday, August 13th, the new buildings were opened to the members.

People acquainted with the neighbourhood of Beswick a few years back, and particularly with Rowsley Street, where the Society's new premises stand, would hardly recognise the district now. Vast changes have been made, and for these the local Co-operative Society may be said to be somewhat responsible. Old landmarks are going, and streets upon streets of respectable working-men's homes now fill their places, while here and there at very regular intervals of space is to be found a branch of the Beswick Co-operative Society. For some twelve years now the inhabitants of Beswick have had a taste of what Co-operation can do, but judging from the remarks overheard on Saturday, last week, there are just a few who are inclined to be wobblers. "However, I think I shall join again," observed one woman, "for I find I cannot get better stuff, with something extra to draw at the quarter end, anywhere else." After all, there can be nothing to despair about the membership of any Society which increases at the rate of 400 in six weeks. And that is Beswick's record since the last branch was opened. All that the Committee wish for is that the members shall be loyal, true Co-operators. "There is need for this," remarked Mr. Chadwick, one of the Committee members, to our representative, for it is often said "that the best day for the private shop-keepers in the neighbourhood is the Co-operative Society's dividend day."

SCENE AT THE OPENING.

It was something to see the aspect of Rowsley Street at the appointed time of opening. An immense crowd of men, women, and children had gathered in front of the new building, and the bedroom windows of the houses on the opposite side of the Stores were crowded with animated faces. There were no decorations to speak of; the Society flag alone indicated the point of concentration. In strict accordance with the programme, a procession was started round the district early in the afternoon, and at four the people sprang smartly to attention, for lively strains of music announced that the wagonette containing the Committee-men and other representatives from neighbouring Societies was returning. The procession was marshalled with the utmost celerity. In the front was an escort of police, following were four horses harnessed to the carriage, and behind were decorated lurries, on which were displayed samples of C.W.S. productions. This may be a convenient place to remark that all along the route Co-operative literature had been distributed.

ADDRESSES IN FRONT OF THE BUILDING.

Mr. Stott and Mr. Chadwick were the big men of the day, but accompanying them were Mr. Brooks, Mr. Worswick, Messrs. Grindrod and Bland (C.W.S. Directors), W. Potts (Bank Department, C.W.S.), W. Wilson, two representatives from the Brightside and Carbrook Society (Sheffield), and many others. As the Committee ascended the platform the crowd fell in its place in front, and without the loss of a moment Mr. Chadwick proceeded to tell of the remarkable progress which Beswick Society had made. They had over 5,000 members, they did a trade of over £100,000 per year, they owned property amounting to £36,000, and this had been depreciated by over £6,000. They had increased their expenses, and he hoped that the members would increase their loyalty, so as to decrease those expenses. After a congratulatory word for Mr. Roddis (the Manager), to whom a great deal of the Beswick Society's success is attributed, Mr. Chadwick asked Mr. Smith (as Architect, and withal a

INTERIOR OF HALL, ROWSLEY STREET, BESWICK.

INTERIOR OF HALL, ROWSLEY STREET, BESWICK.

well-known Co-operator, and twice Mayor of Eccles) to make a presenta-
tion of a gold watch to Mr. Stott. This over, the audience applauded,
and Mr. Stott returned thanks, remarking that so long as he lived he, a
working man himself, hoped to do his best for the working men—nay, and
women, too, added Mr. Stott—of Beswick. He was indeed truly proud
of their eleven branches, their five butchery shops, and their two drapery
and boot shops. The building they were about to open was not a bit too
grand for the working men and women of Beswick. He only hoped that the
members would make use of the building, for up to the present they had
had no hall in which they could air their grievances. The new premises
would prove a rich heritage for their members' children and their
children's children. Amidst ringing cheers, the premises were duly
declared open. But before the gathering dispersed Mr. Bland came to
the front of the platform and, in moving a vote of thanks to the speakers,
remarked that he had for the first time that afternoon traversed over the
Beswick district. He was delighted with what the Beswick people had
done, and it was amazing to think what they had done in so short a time.
The Committee had gone right amongst the people, and he was pleased
that the grand new premises were placed in the midst of the people.
Mr. Carlyle (the builder) briefly seconded the resolution.

EVERYBODY AND EVERYTHING IN FORM.

It should be mentioned that charming weather favoured the opening,
and the men and women, many of whom were in their working clothes,
were most amiable. Of young Co-operators there were legions, and, as
usual, they were to the front. Another happy circumstance is the fact
that the opening could be made under architectural completeness. Thanks
chiefly to Mr. Walsingham (the Architect) and the Manager in the new
shop, our representative was able to get an early inspection of the
premises. The site on which the new premises stand was bought outright
by the Society some six years ago, and already about half of the land has
been covered with the Society's bakery and stables, while now the front
portion is covered by the new buildings. When space and light are so
costly as they are to-day, the Beswick people must congratulate themselves upon the possession of their halls and shops, where every allowance
possible has been made for light, space, and air. The heating and
ventilation of halls is always a serious problem, as many Co-operators
are aware ; but the Beswick Co-operators seem to have got the results of
a study of many Co-operative Societies' experiences and requirements.
An arrangement has been made whereby all the rooms and the large hall,
which will seat 1,000 people, are heated by warm filtered fresh air. The
apparatus is fixed in the basement, quite separate from anything else.
Cold air is drawn in from the yard, and passes through a filter which
can be washed. After being filtered it (the air) is carried through a steam
heating battery, and propelled into all the rooms by an electric fan. By
disusing the heating battery the same fan in hot weather will force cool,
clean air into all the rooms. And, so as to ensure a sufficiency of heat
when needed, a series of radiators heated by steam from the boiler has
also been fixed, and the persons occupying certain rooms have absolute
control over the temperature. All foul air is abstracted by ducts and
flues, which are connected with a large duct over the hall ceiling, whence
it is carried into an ornamental turret on the roof.

THE BUILDINGS THEMSELVES.

Everything has been carried out from an artistic and scientific stand-point.   Mosaic concrete has been used for the flooring of the main entrance and for the landings.   The general offices are at the main entrance, and alongside are the grocery, furniture, and crockery shops. Under these are well-lighted basements, with walls lined wlth glazed bricks and with wood block floors.   Extreme cleanliness was to be observed everywhere, and every precaution seemed to have been taken to avoid all dampness.   Over the shops is the large public hall, with sundry smaller rooms, including a kitchen, where a hot and cold water supply has been laid on.   In a room over the kitchen there is a specially designed tea-making gas-heated apparatus.   There are two exits from the hall, both leading direct to the street level.   All the landings are made of fire-resisting material, and are panelled with tiles.   Just fronting the entrance to the hall on the landing are two stained-glass windows, which are very effective, whether seen on going up the staircase or from the hall. The walls of the large hall are just colour washed in artistic duresco tints. There are windows along one side and end, and a series of dormer windows in the roof, which can be opened when necessary.   The façade of the building is built of red Accrington bricks, with dressings of buff and terra-cotta introduced.   It will be an easy matter to wash the surfaces of these bricks at any time, and in Manchester such a provision is very necessary if a building is to retain its brightness.   There are electric lights throughout the building, with gas piping for emergency.   By all these improvements Beswick Society will assuredly become one of the most up-to-date and enterprising Societies in Lancashire.   It should be added that the whole of the buildings and fixtures have been carried out under the superintendence of Mr. Arthur H. Walsingham, of the firm of Messrs. Smith, Walsingham, and Smith, Manchester, who also designed the bakery adjoining.   The cost of the new block is about £9,000.

"We must have loyalty" was the command of the Chairman at the evening meeting.   Certainly the Beswick women Co-operators never looked more in earnest than they did on Saturday at the new shop.   "And it is the very best of everything that they buy," observed the head shopman.

The concert was a great success, the C.W.S. Male Voice Choir being encored again and again.

PAYMENT OF DIVIDEND.

With the inception of new offices, convenient of access to all our members in every district, it was decided that in future all members' dividends, except City office members, should be paid at the General Offices.   This, however, did not meet with the general approval of the members at first, and instead a trial was made in the payment of dividend at the two new premises and two outside branches.   This went on for some time, until it was found absolutely necessary to reorganise the system, and it was proved conclusively that the objection of members living at a distance to journeying to Rowsley Street for dividends had no serious foundation.   A large number of those members came to Rowsley Street on the first dividend day, although provision was made for their district on a later date, thus creating a congestion at the General Offices, and a difficulty in the attention given.   At the time it was considered advisable to reorganise the system some 2,200 members had been paid dividend on the first of dividend days, and consequently the other days were hardly necessary.   It was then agreed to adopt the original intention of the Committee: to centralise the payment of dividends at the General Offices by arrangement of numbers.   This course has since been in vogue, and has proved an undoubted success, there being no waste of time by the members, with more staff to cope with the business, no anxiety, and everything running smoothly ; the extra distance of journey being compensated for by the facilities at hand for dealing with the requirements and the saving of time and worry.

EDUCATIONAL WORK.

The General Committee on August 19th formed themselves into an Educational and Recreative Committee to carry on the educational work of the Society.   A syllabus was arranged for the coming winter of lectures, concerts, &c.   A grant of £20 was made by the members on August 22nd so that the Committee could carry on the work without interference with current accounts, and subsequent grants have been made at almost every Quarterly Meeting since.

The response to the various features was rather discouraging, the greatest attendance being at the children's concerts.   Still, it was hoped that 1905 would be better, but that season's experience was similar.   A better response was, however, experienced in 1906, when the programme contained some changes, and another attempt is being made for 1907–8 with a similar programme, and it is hoped the result will justify a continuance of the educational work. Of course, it is true we have to compete with the many attractions existent in Manchester, which probably is accountable for our non-success, but if our members only knew the good things that are provided no doubt there would be better attendances—a visit would impress, and we live in hopes.

PLATE GLASS INSURANCE.

A plate glass insurance fund was formed with £10 on August 22nd, with the view to gradually building up a fund so that we might become our own insurers of the shop windows, and thus save premiums annually paid to companies. We now have all the windows insured in our own fund, and with the small risks, occasional grants, and the payment of premiums—which had grown to a large sum annually—into the fund, we have now a reserve of ample proportions that will be able to meet many risks.

The members also on August 22nd increased the remuneration of the Committee for their services to 2s. 6d. per meeting, the same amount to be paid for Sub-Committee meetings, believing that their extra duties deserved better recognition by increased remuneration.

REMOVAL OF OGDEN STREET PREMISES.

About May the Committee were compelled to consider the condition of Ogden Street premises, the lease of which would expire at Christmas. It was thought undesirable to continue business in these premises longer than was absolutely necessary owing to the bad condition they had been allowed to get into by the landlord for want of proper repair. We had had a lot of trouble with the landlord previously in regard to repairs, and considered we had had enough. The Committee, in viewing the district for suitable premises, came across a shop at 54, Union Street, which was the only available means of transferring the business, the price of various plots of land in the vicinity being too exorbitant. The tenant of the shop stated a price for his goodwill and fixtures, which was considered reasonable ; but before a settlement was come to the Committee approached the Directors of the Manchester and Salford Society w:th the object of obtaining their permission to establish ourselves at this address, as it was at no great distance from their

No. 7 BRANCH, 54, UNION STREET, ARDWICK.

Central premises.   It was pointed out that we had great difficulty in securing a shop other than this, for the transfer of our Ogden Street business was absolutely necessary. They, however, took a friendly view of our situation, and stated that they had no objection to the transfer of our business to the address named.

A lease of tenancy was arranged, and, after various structural alterations had been carried out and internal fixtures put in, the shop was opened for business on December 8th.

AUDITOR.

Mr. Ashhurst, Auditor to the Society, tendered his resignation to the Quarterly Meeting held on November 28th, due to the advice of his doctor that he must give up all extra duties if he desired to regain his usual health.   He very much regretted having to sever his connection as an official of the Society after so many years of office, but hoped at some future time to rejoin us in our work.   The Committee expressed their regrets that Mr. Ashhurst should be compelled to terminate his official duties, but hoped he would soon recover good health.   The members also accepted his resignation, at the same time tendering regrets that he was compelled to take this step in consequence of ill-health, but hoped he might be speedily restored to again take up some official work in connection with the Society.   They further tendered to him their sincere thanks for the very valuable assistance rendered to the Society, formerly in the capacity of Secretary, and subsequently as Auditor.   The vacancy was filled at the same meeting in the person of Mr. R. S. Clark.

THE UNEMPLOYED.

The labour market was in a very bad state about November, and to the Lord Mayor's fund for the benefit of the unemployed almost everybody were contributing—associations, manufacturers, tradesmen, and the employés of those concerns—such was the sympathy extant for these unfortunate people, and the utmost efforts were put forth to find them employment.

L

This Society, like many other institutions, promoted a concert in our Hall for the benefit of the fund, and everyone worked right willingly to make it a success.   Our thanks are due to the members of the Ancoats University Settlement for the able assistance they rendered in the arranging and providing of artistes for a portion of the programme ; also to the artistes for their kind services.   Everything was given gratuitously to the object, and as a result of the concert, which was held on December 17th, £11. 18s. 6d. was handed over to the Lord Mayor's Unemployed Fund.   The Society also gave fifty 2lb. loaves of bread weekly for eight weeks to the Bradford Ward Distress Committee's Relief Fund.

CHAPTER IX.

1905.

CONFERENCE.

Our Society invited the Manchester District Co-operative Association for the first time to hold its next conference in our premises at Rowsley Street, as previously the Society had not an opportunity of extending such an invitation for want of a suitable meeting room. The invitation was accepted, and a conference was held on Saturday, January 14th, when Mr. J. C. Gray, J.P., General Secretary to the Co-operative Union, submitted his paper: "Notes of Importance to Committees and Officials." The delegates were afterwards entertained to tea, and the Society received hearty thanks from them for the hospitality.

SUGAR TAX.

On January 30th a resolution was sent to the Right Hon. A. J. Balfour, M.P., the Chancellor of the Exchequer, and the *Co-operative News*, relative to the existing Sugar Tax, in the following terms :—

That the Co-operators of the North-Western Section, consisting of 851,085 members of 509 Societies, emphatically condemn the Sugar Convention, which prevents the importation into this country of cheap sugar, the result of which is to largely increase the cost of an article of important domestic use, and to limit its supply with disastrous effects to our industries. Further, they are of opinion that the tax imposed on sugar for the purposes of the late war in South Africa should be repealed, as such taxation is a great hardship on the poorer classes of the community, with whom sugar is one of the principal articles of household consumption. They, therefore, call upon the Government to repeal the war tax on sugar, and to renounce the convention at the earliest possible moment.

BRANCH OF WOMEN'S GUILD.

On January 30th the Committee were invited by Mrs. Eddie, of the Women's Co-operative Guild, to form a branch of their Guild in connection with this Society, in the event of which she would render all the assistance she could in its formation by providing speakers and giving advice as to its management and objects. The Committee replied that they could not see their way at this juncture to support a branch, as we had no funds available to draw upon for this object, the educational work being carried on by the General Committee from special grants made by the members, as the current accounts would allow. They were also of opinion that the time was not opportune to promote a branch in connection with our Society. However, the matter was taken up by the members themselves, as a member sent in the following notice of motion to the Quarterly Meeting, February 27th, for consideration : " That the time has now arrived for the formation of a Women's Guild in connection with the Beswick Co-operative Society Limited." The motion was considered, and in its support the mover submitted that a branch of the Guild could do good work amongst our members by influencing the sale of our goods and the introduction of new members. They could also do good by arranging socials, lectures, picnics, &c., and so bring members more together. The branch would be no source of expense to the Society, as it would be made self-supporting.

Although the proposal met with opposition it was ultimately carried into effect. Subsequently a meeting to inaugurate a branch was called for April 4th in the rooms at Ashton Old Road, but the attendance was only a poor response to the announcements made, as, in addition to the Committee and their wives, there would only be about a dozen members to meet Mrs. Eddie, who was present to state the aims and objects of the Guild and put the branch on a business footing. About 20 members were enrolled, inclusive of gentlemen who were only enrolled as honorary members ; Mrs. Stott was elected President, Mrs. Green, Hon. Secretary, and Mrs. Ogden, Hon. Treasurer. The branch has added considerably to its ranks since the inaugural meeting, and has held many lectures, socials, &c., since that time. The funds have been added to by the members in Quarterly Meeting to the extent of £15.

VINCENT STREET BRANCH.

On April 7th our Architect, Mr. Walsingham, submitted sketches of a proposed grocery shop to be erected on the Society's vacant land in Vincent Street, Higher Openshaw, to the Committee, who made a selection. It was now considered

No. 11 BRANCH, VINCENT STREET, HIGHER OPENSHAW.

opportune to cater for the wants of this district, and thus relieve the congestion at our Mill Street Branch.   Tenders were invited, and the contract was given to Messrs. Wooller and Sons, of Eccles, for the sum of £938.   The work was commenced forthwith, and completed by the end of November.   Announcement was made of the opening ceremony and an invitation given to the residents to attend a grand free concert in celebration of the event.   The concert was held in the Whitworth Hall, Openshaw, and was a great success.   There was a capital musical programme, and several rousing speeches were made by the President and members of the Committee.

The new premises were opened for business on December 1st, the formal opening ceremony taking place on Saturday, December 2nd.   The honour of performing the ceremony was given to Mr. T. Chadwick, member of the Committee. Mr. E. Taylor acted as Chairman, and they were supported on the platform by other members of the Committee, officials, architect, contractor, and representatives from neighbouring Societies.   A procession had been made from the Central premises, Rowsley Street, accompanied by a brass band, and handbills advertising the Society were distributed *en route*.   A large number of persons joined the Society with the opening, and the trade that has since been done proves the justification for its establishment.

The following appeared in the "Wheatsheaf" and *Co-operative News* :—

Our new branch at Vincent Street was opened on December 2nd. The ceremony, which was presided over by Mr. Taylor (Committee), was witnessed by a large gathering of members and friends.

The Chairman, in the course of a short address, said the Committee had invited the members to be present on that occasion in order that they might see for themselves their new premises.   The Branch Store they were about to open was an example of what working men could do by combination, and he appealed to those who were not members of the Society to join at once.   It would only cost sixpence, and he could assure them that the benefits to be derived from the Co-operative movement were many. He spoke from personal experience when he said that, and they were as much entitled to those benefits as he himself was.   The working classes had the future in their own hands, and one of the best and greatest agencies for improving their lot was the Co-operative movement.

Mr. Wooller (Messrs. Wooller and Sons, Eccles) was the next speaker. He said he had been a Co-operator for about thirty-five years, and for twenty-five years he never withdrew a single penny of his dividend. The consequence was that he accumulated over £100 in the Society to which he belonged, and he could assure them that that money had come in very handy indeed. Mr. Wooller also spoke kindly words to the children, and expressed the hope that the Society would always look after the rising generation.

Mr. Walsingham (Messrs. Smith, Walsingham, and Smith, Architects), who has now been connected with the erection of fifty-four Co-operative shops, followed. He said he was interested in some surrounding property, and could bear testimony to the fact that the best tenants were Co-operators. Mr. Walsingham afterwards presented Mr. T. Chadwick (member of the Committee, to whom fell the honour of opening the branch) with an ornamented key as a souvenir of the occasion.

Opening the Branch.

Mr. Chadwick thanked Mr. Walsingham for his gift, and his colleagues for conferring upon him the honour of opening the new branch—an honour which, he could assure them, he was very proud of. The erection and the fitting up of the branch had cost about £1,200, and he thought they would agree that great credit was due to the architect and the builder for the way in which they had carried out the work. He considered the members of the Society living in that district were very loyal members, on the whole, and the Committee, to show their appreciation of such loyalty, had placed those new premises in their midst. The neighbouring branch at Mill Street had become congested on account of increasing business, and the new branch would not only relieve it a little, but would help the Society to build up a trade in a new district. The people round about evidently appreciated the action of the Committee in opening a branch in that street, and in proof of this he stated that between 70 and 80 new members had already been made. Referring to the Society generally, he said its progress had been remarkable. The Chairman had already given them some figures to show how the Society had grown in 13 years, and perhaps they would also like to know that the Society had now 23 branches, a Coal Department, a Bakery, and two large Public Halls. Mr. Chadwick then dealt with Co-operation from a general point of view, and said it had been stated that if there were no dividends there would be no Co-operators. His reply to that was, if there were no profits there would be no shopkeepers. Again, it was stated that Co-operators were selfish, and thought only of themselves. but he quoted several instances to show that the statement was incorrect, notably when there was an engineering dispute in the district. He closed his remarks by appealing to non-members to join the Society, and said by so doing they would not only be helping themselves, but mankind generally. He then opened the shop for business, and wished it a prosperous career.

Mr. Stott (President of the Society) moved a vote of thanks to the Chairman, which was seconded by Mr. Brooks, and suitably replied to by Mr. Taylor. Mr. Stott made one point perfectly clear, that, in asking for members, they did not desire anyone to leave a neighbouring Society in order to become members of the Beswick Society,

The proceedings then terminated.

Compliments.

The Manager on October 2nd submitted to the Committee the following testimonial, unsolicited, from a party who had had a tea catered for them in our Hall, which speaks for itself :—

42, Whitworth Street,

Dear Sirs,   Manchester, September 28th, 1905.

We, the undersigned, beg to express, on behalf of the employés of Messrs. Somerset and Co. Ltd., our sincere thanks to you for the capable manner in which you catered for our party on Saturday last, September 23rd. The excellent meat tea which you provided for us has given general satisfaction, and the manner in which it was served is deserving of our best commendation. We also desire to thank you for the arrangement of the refreshment bar for our convenience, the refreshments provided being of the best quality and at very moderate prices. We wish to say also that the general arrangements and up-to-date contrivances which you possess at Rowsley Street Hall render it an ideal place for social gatherings such as ours, and these advantages, together with the beautiful interior of the hall, deserve to be more widely known.

On behalf of the employés, most sincerely yours,

T. H. Kelly, Manager.
W. T. Harwood,
Wm. H. Nolan, } Hon. Secs.

Mr. Roddis, Beswick Co-operative Society.

The Committee in October decided to meet the whole of the Managers in conference quarterly, for the discussion of the published balance sheet, and an interchange of views on various matters of business for the ultimate progression of the Society.

Cocoa Lecture.

The most successful lecture held in the Society's Hall in connection with the Society was a cocoa lecture on November 20th, under the auspices of the Beswick Women's Guild and the Society. The attendance was exceptional, a large number of people having to be turned away for want of accommodation, the Hall being packed with 800 or more people. In addition to the interesting lecture, illustrated with lantern slides, given by Mr. Turner, of the C.W.S., samples of cocoa and chocolate were distributed amongst the audience. Cups of C.W.S. Broma Cocoa were also handed round, with samples of C.W.S. Biscuits. The lecturer, although encouraged by the large gathering, was bound to admit that it was like taking coals to Newcastle (for a simile) bringing C.W.S. Cocoa before the Beswick members, as Beswick Society dealt in none other practically but C.W.S. Cocoas.

CHAPTER X.

—

1906.

On March 19th Mr. G. Beresford, 72, Grey Mare Lane, arranged with the Committee to repair and tune pianos for our members at a nominal fee. Many members have taken advantage of this arrangement to have their instruments over-hauled and put into proper pitch, and it is hoped it will become more widely known. Mr. Care, Beswick Studio, Ashton New Road, also arranged to supply our members with high-class photos at reasonable prices, and this arrangement should appeal to many. Full dividend is allowed on accounts with both gentlemen.

CO-OPERATIVE CONVALESCENT HOMES ASSOCIATION.

The members in Quarterly Meeting on May 28th decided unanimously to become members of the North-Western Co-operative Convalescent Homes Association, and to take up 153 £1 shares. The shares were paid out of the reserve fund, so that they do not appear in our accounts as assets. The Homes are situated at Blackpool and Otley, and they have been of great benefit to many of our members already. Others have the same privilege if they will take advantage of the opportunity, as they exist solely for Co-operators. Recommends can be obtained at the General Office.

A fund was created at the above meeting with £20 for the purpose of insuring all our employees, except those using machinery, against claims for compensation arising out of accidents, and it has now grown to over £200. The Society has been very fortunate up to now in not having experienced any claims of this nature, but one never knows what will happen. The formation of this fund retains the increasing premiums, instead of paying them to other companies.

BRANCHES REQUESTED.

The Committee continue to receive requisitions from members and friends in outside districts for the establishment of branches, but it is not always possible at the moment to meet their wishes.   The Committee are always on the look-out for suitable positions for business.

We are doing our best to cater for the wishes of our Stuart Street friends, who have been assiduous in their pressure for a branch for some years ; and our Butler Street members will be provided with a Butchery Department when occasion presents itself.   The members at the extreme end of Bradford Road district have wanted a branch for some years, and it is expected one will be established in the near future.

A large number of people, members and those most anxious to join us, in the Longsight area are very persistent in their request for a branch.   It is a problem that is not easily solved, and I am afraid it is almost impossible beyond our present delivery system.   We hope, however, that those who are anxious to join us do not remain outside the movement because we fail in this respect, though it would give us the greatest pleasure to supply the convenience.

On August 27th the Society lost the services of Mr. Clark, who was compelled to relinquish his duties as auditor owing to his removal out of town.   He was tendered sincere regrets from the Committee and members for his resignation, and their thanks for his past services.   Mr. Ashhurst was unanimously appointed to link up his past valuable services as auditor in the vacancy.

PARKER STREET.

The Committee took into consideration, about May, the advisability of rebuilding our Parker Street premises, which had been cleared out of the assets.   The premises had become altogether too small and inconvenient for the business transacted, so that plans for new premises were drawn out by our architect.   Messrs. Wooller and Sons (Eccles) secured the contract for about £1,200, and proceeded with the alteration. The business was continued during alterations, and when the upper portion was dismantled, and only the shop remained, it resembled the " little wooden hut."   Whilst the old building was diminishing and the new one rising our members who

No. 3 BRANCH, PARKER STREET.
(Now Rebuilt.)

traded at this branch suffered some inconvenience, and we, therefore, feel greatly indebted to them for their indulgence in the circumstances.   The new building fully compensates us for the trouble by the greater facilities for doing a larger business, and is a building of which we are proud.   It was not thought necessary to have a re-opening ceremony on December 20th, but it stands as a permanent ornament and attraction to the district.

Boot repairing was undertaken for our members in September by a neighbouring Society, who arranged to execute our orders until such time that we could commence ourselves. The response up to now has not warranted such a course being adopted, but we hope that before long it will be found necessary.   We are very desirous of supplying all the wants of our members, and trust they will not forget us when requiring work of this nature.   Good work is guaranteed, at reasonable prices with full dividend allowed.

GREATER MANCHESTER SOCIETY.

A very important question arose in September, when a suggestion was made by Mr. J. C. Gray (of the Co-operative Union) that we should meet jointly with the Pendleton and Manchester and Salford Societies for the consideration of amalgamated effort in Manchester.   The first of a series of conferences was held on November 30th, when Mr. Gray submitted his scheme for the furtherance of Co-operative effort in Manchester.   The question eventually resolved itself into a condensed form of Mr. Gray's Congress proposal for a National Co-operative Society, by merging the three Societies into one.   Many points were brought out, good, bad, and indifferent, during discussions at subsequent conferences, and it was eventually decided to reduce the constitution of the Committees for more minute deliberation to a Joint Committee of twelve members—four from each Society.   The Joint Committee have almost finished their consideration of so important a question, and will then submit the result to a joint conference of the three Societies' Committees.   If, however, they decide to favour the proposal, it will require the ratification of the members of each Society.   The question is a very important and complicated one, and will require much consideration prior to adoption.

Closing the year 1906 I cannot do better than append my annual report of the year's business, which was published with the programme of the annual tea party, held in January, 1907.

To THE MEMBERS,

It is again my privilege and pleasure to submit to you a review of another successful year of trading. My last report was of the year ending October 16th, 1905 (a period of 53 weeks), and now present figures for the year ending October 15th, 1906 (of 52 weeks). Although the various increases do not show the immensity recorded last year, yet it is one of satisfaction to know that there has been substantial increases in some departments, and for the whole not a single decrease.

Therefore we still remain on the highway of progression, and it gives much encouragement to those responsible to you for the results.

I would like to say here that, besides grocery, there are other departments deserving of your support, and if you would loyally trade at those departments better results could be shown at the year's end ; and it is to your benefit to do so, because the shops, like the Society, belong to you, and, therefore, our success is your success.

I have dissected the various accounts for the year, so that they may appear before you in a condensed form, and save you the necessity of traversing through the past balance sheets to obtain an idea of the Society's sound financial position. It should also serve as a useful lever in the inducement of your friends to become members of so forward a Society.

SALES.—The sales for the 52 weeks have amounted to £135,798, a further record, exceeding the previous year's total by £10,327. It is a splendid increase, and accounted for as follows :—

	£				£
Grocery	88,892,	increase over last year	5,490
Direct Purchases	16,204	,,	,,	,,	1,038
Drapery and Tailoring	8,487	,,	,,	,,	782
Boots and Shoes	2,654	,,	,,	,,	103
Furnishing	1,786	,,	,,	,,	400
Butchering	10,488	,,	,,	,,	1,741
Coal	7,287	,,	,,	,,	173
Bakery Productions ..	8,976	,,	,,	,,	503

Average weekly sales, £2,612, an increase over last year of £245.

It is specially interesting to note the great increase in the Butchering Department, which shows £700 greater than the previous year's increase. This department, like all our others, only offers the best quality of goods, and, therefore, should appeal to those who wish to have only the best and purest of foodstuffs. It is a significant fact that Co-operative Societies owe their advancement in no small degree to the supplying of pure goods.

EXPENSES have an important bearing upon Societies' results, and I am pleased to say that ours have been reduced 1¼d. per £ over last year. The total cost of distribution was £12,033, or equal to 1s. 9¼d. per £ of the sales. The production expenses have been £1,097. You must, however, bear in mind that these items include interest on share capital, and depreciation of buildings, &c.

PROFITS.—The net balance resulting from trade, disposable to the members, amounted to £19,982 ; equal to 2s. 11¼d. per £ of sales, and an increase of £2,419 over last year. In addition, the sum of £1,562 has been apportioned to members as interest on their share capital.

The balance was divided as follows :—

	£
Dividend to Members on their purchases, at 2s. 9d. in the £	18,081
Bonus to Employés of the Society	183
Donations to Charities, &c.	40
Extra Depreciation of Buildings, Fixtures, &c.	536
Reserve Fund	400
Educational Purposes Fund	140
Special Repairs Fund	80
Employés' Compensation Insurance Fund	60
Plate Glass Insurance Fund	30
Dividend Equalisation Fund	432
	£19,982

In addition to the above £112 has been paid to members for checks they were unable to leave to rank for dividend, owing to their compulsory removal out of town, and £5 paid to non-members, out of the gross balance.

PURCHASES.—The Society purchased goods to the value of £104,592, of which 88¾ per cent grocery, 94¾ per cent drapery, 94 per cent furnishing, and 100 per cent each tailoring and boots have been supplied by the C.W.S. There is not much room for improvement in our loyalty to the C.W.S., as everything where possible is purchased from them. You may rest assured also that no goods are sold by us that have not been produced under fair conditions of labour, the Committee being strong advocates for the abolition of sweating.

MEMBERSHIP.—The addition to the membership roll has been a considerable one, totalling 1,934 new members. It is a matter for regret that 1,453 members have been compelled to sever their connection, but of this number 981 have removed their place of residence too far out of our district to remain purchasing members. The remainder are due to various causes, some through circumstances beyond their control. The number of members, therefore, on October 15th, was 6,468. I would again take this opportunity of inviting new adherents to our movement ; which, if they once thoroughly understand, they will never be outside. Members would assist our progress by introducing our Society to their friends.

CAPITAL.—The members have to their credit in share capital £38,633, which is an increase of £6,632 over last year. Members would serve their interests by making contributions to their share account. Better interest

M

cannot be obtained on their investment elsewhere. We pay 5 per cent per annum on sums up to £75, and 3½ per cent per annum over that amount up to £200, provided purchases are made in accordance with the rules. The members' capital is securely invested in land, buildings, fixtures, rolling stock, goods, shares, and loans. The accounts are certified quarterly by qualified auditors appointed by the members to see that everything is conducted in a proper manner, and a glance at the quarterly balance sheet will convince the most sceptical of the financial soundness of your Society.

PENNY BANK.—The number of depositors in the Small Savings Bank remains at that given last year, viz., 5,375. A great number of new depositors have opened accounts, but were given numbers that had previously lapsed through various causes. It is surprising to find that £5,521 has been placed on deposit during the year, and the sum of £4,720 withdrawn, leaving capital belonging to depositors of £4,759, an increase of £927 over last year. Interest to the extent of £127 has been added to deposit accounts, a rate of 3½ per cent per annum.

LAND, BUILDINGS, FIXTURES, &c.—This account contains some of the best assets of the Society, owing to the manner of depreciation during past years. What originally cost £41,267 now stands at £30,857, a total depreciation of £10,410. The value of depreciation is well known, and should, therefore, be encouraged. The additions during the year were £1,846, and the gradual depreciation amounted to £1,700, which, with extra £536, makes a total of £2,236.

RESERVES.—One striking feature in the balance sheet that should not be overlooked is the reserve for contingencies, amounting to £2,496. The reserve fund of £1,202 is separately invested with the C.W.S., and the other items are for an equally useful purpose, the largest of which is the dividend equalisation fund of £1,006.

EDUCATIONAL.—During the year the Committee have promoted the following events for the social and intellectual recreation of our members and their children :—

The Annual Tea Party was held on two dates, as last year, owing to insufficient accommodation for the number attending, viz., January 20th and 27th ; 400 persons sat down to tea, catered by the General Manager, on the first date, and 370 on the second, or a total of 770.

On February 8th a free Lecture-Concert was held and was well attended. Mr. Pollitt (Eccles) delivered his lecture on "Co-operation : What it is, and what we mean by it."

Children's Concerts are always popular, and 730 children were present on February 21st, Miss Pennington providing the entertainment ; and at the Concert held on November 7th, when Prof. Le Mare gave his Punch and Judy, Conjuring, Ventriloquial, and other performances, 840 children attended.

Social Evenings were held on two occasions ; the one on October 4th was held jointly with the Beswick Women's Guild, and was very successful. The number being limited, 260 persons took part in dancing. The same could not be said of the one held on December 20th, owing to counteracting influences so near Christmas, only about 60 responding to the announcement.

A Grand Concert was held on March 15th, and although a capital programme was given by the C.W.S. Male Voice Choir, they were much discouraged by only having an audience of 210. It was a treat specially arranged, but evidently not fully appreciated.

A very interesting experiment was made on December 4th, when the Committee invited the male members and lady members' husbands to a Smoking Concert. Everything was provided free, and about 500 responded. Samples of C.W.S. tobacco, with matches, were distributed to all present. Mr. Morrison's Concert Party supplied a good programme, and the President (Mr. Stott) gave a rousing address on " Trade Unionism and Co-operation." This event should be productive of good results for the Society.

On Whit Saturday, June 9th, the Committee arranged an Excursion to Morecambe for the members, and guaranteed 300 tickets, but only 270 availed themselves of the trip, so a loss ensued. It was a very pleasurable outing, as those who went will testify. A breakfast was catered by the Lancaster Co-operative Society, and reduced admission to the piers, &c., was arranged.

The Children's Field Day, held on July 21st, was the usual success, and the weather similarly favoured us. There were 3,600 ticket holders, and, augmented with the general influx of interested people and outsiders, the gathering would number 5,000. The workers had to get through the usual programme of races, and supply refreshment. The prizes given to the winners of the races were exceptionally good, and our thanks are given to the C.W.S. employés for their present of special prizes for winners' races. Entertainments were also provided.

GENERAL.—The Society did not make any further extension of business beyond the new branch in Vincent Street, Openshaw, referred to in my last report, if one may except, however, the rebuilding of Parker Street premises. The business at Parker Street was continued during alterations under great inconvenience, and we are indebted to those members who met the wishes of the Committee by sending their orders to the Central. The rebuilding had become absolutely necessary, and on December 20th substantial and handsome premises were completed to facilitate a growing trade.

The amount spent in our departments through the Clothing Club was £3,428, an increase over last year of £662. The weekly subscription is only 1s. for a £1 share, but the shares are not limited. Members should join and have the benefit of the Club.

The General Club, previously used for the purpose of preparing for the Christmas festivities, will, in future, be in operation throughout the year. By this means members will have an opportunity of putting away moneys they do not require at the moment for some future occasion. Any amount will be received, whether much or little, and it is hoped every advantage will be taken of this new arrangement. The coupons may be spent in any department, and one should find it of the utmost utility in making purchases in the Furnishing Department. The amount spent at Christmas through this club was about £400.

Our sales in Bonus Tea have increased the turnover of some of our other departments to the extent of £570. The value of the checks given with the tea is 10d. per lb., for which 10d. per lb. extra has been paid. This arrangement finds favour with many of our members, who, instead of going to the present-giving shops, keep their trade with us, and know the value they are obtaining. It is the means of securing necessary articles that would not be purchased in any other manner.

I would again draw your attention to the fact that it is important that those members who have much capital in the Society should nominate at the Office some person to whom their shares should be paid in case of decease. Many difficulties may arise if this course is neglected.

Members would oblige if, when changing their residence, they would intimate the fact, along with their share number, so that our register may be duly corrected.

I also wish to point out that the Society is in the position to supply recommends to three Convalescent Homes: Roden, Blackpool, and Otley; the charge at each being 12s. 6d. per week. Further information I shall be pleased to supply upon application.

In conclusion, I am happy to state that the trade for the quarter just ended has reached the record total of over £36,000. There appears to be every prospect of a continuance of the recent good trade in the district, and I sincerely hope such will be the case. The markets are easing somewhat, and should consequently benefit the consumer. I trust the members will not forget us in their affluence, but deal loyally with each department of the Society's business, so that your Society may progress beyond expectancy, and also give support to new ventures—for instance, the Boot Repairing, which is now only in its experimental stage.

I append my usual tabulation, showing at a glance the remarkable progress made during the past 14 years.

Wishing that the ensuing year may be a prosperous one to every member of the Society, and may produce a still more brilliant report for the Society at its close,

I have the honour to remain,

A. E. WORSWICK, *Secretary.*

January, 1907.

PROGRESS OF THE SOCIETY FOR FOURTEEN YEARS
ENDING JULY, 1906.

Year.	Sales.			Dividend.			Interest.			Share Capital.			Members.
	£	s.	d.	£	s.	d.	£	s.	d.	£	s.	d.	
*1893	3583	4	8½	124	4	0	17	3	2	456	12	10	147
1894	5715	5	2	408	3	8	23	19	0	629	12	2	357
1895	8442	18	0	797	12	8	31	14	2	971	12	3	513
†1896	13524	9	8	1542	9	6	52	16	10	1173	18	6	904
‡1897	21543	4	10½	2965	15	2	68	17	2	2090	3	3	1336
1898	29230	5	8	3801	12	1	118	6	6	4123	1	2	1770
1899	38514	7	2	5056	4	8	218	10	11	6446	19	3	2220
1900	50930	1	6	7014	0	10	314	3	10	8904	16	9	2938
1901	63123	11	9	8603	18	1	447	9	0	11628	11	10	3339
1902	70912	3	10	9359	12	6	516	16	3	13842	9	11	3629
1903	89524	12	5	11953	7	3	706	0	9	18624	11	10	4254
1904	99893	7	3	13295	14	4	944	13	9	23795	8	4	5043
*1905	124496	0	9	16664	6	5	1191	4	0	30377	5	0	5926
1906	131342	9	4	17804	18	10	1486	7	0	37298	6	4	6325
TOTAL.	750776	2	1	99392	0	0	6138	2	4	37298	6	4	6325
INCREASE over first year	127759	4	7½	17680	14	10	1469	3	10	36841	13	6	6178

* 53 weeks. † 55 weeks. ‡ 51 weeks.

1907.

DEATH OF OUR PRESIDENT.

On January 21st various members of the Committee and officials were shocked to hear of the unexpected death of our esteemed President (Mr. G. E. Stott). The news came as a severe blow to us, which meant a serious loss, and it was also felt by other bodies, so great was he held in respect by all shades of opinion. Many letters of condolence in our loss were received from our friends. The Committee, officials, employés, and members of the Society tendered their deepest sympathy to Mrs. Stott and family in their sad bereavement. It was also placed on record the very valuable services Mr. Stott rendered the Society during his long tenure of office.

Our establishments were closed for the funeral on January 24th, and the interment was attended by a full representation of the Society, and also by representatives from other institutions.

Mr. William Brooks (of the Committee) was elected to the Presidency on February 25th, and his vacancy was filled by Mr. W. Alcock.

NEW STABLES.

Very opportune came the knowledge to the Committee in February of the City Corporation's intention to sell the Bradford tram stables by auction, as we were in very urgent need of more stabling accommodation, and on the look out for suitable land. It was decided without hesitation to make a bid for the property, which would be of the utmost utility to us ; so that a survey was made and a valuation got out by our architect. Our solicitors examined the conditions of sale, and found nothing to deter us from securing the property if at all possible. There were 1,987 square yards, upon which the only real chief payable was £12. 16s., an overriding chief being fully indemnified. Our architect undertook the purchase on our behalf at the auction, and it is pleasant to record that his final bid of £1,050 secured the property. The property could have been resold immediately afterwards at a handsome profit. The members ratified the purchase in meeting on February 25th, and it was afterwards completed. Many extensions of our business are now possible with this valuable acquisition, and which will occupy the attention of the Committee for some time to come.

The employés were again thoughtfully considered by the Committee in March, when it was decided that, in future, all male employés, when they reach the age of 21, no matter what their duties are, shall be paid not less than the Co-operative Employés' Union minimum rate of wages, viz., 24s. per week, thereby raising the standard of many employés payable under different unions. The Committee also decided to reduce the shop hours of all establishments on Thursdays to 7-30 p.m. ; and on Saturdays, Grocery and Furnishing Departments to 7 p.m. ; Drapery, Boots, Tailoring, and Butchery Departments to 7-30 p.m.

Co-operative Union Limited.

The members in Quarterly Meeting on May 13th unanimously decided to subscribe our quota, viz., £81. 7s. 6d., towards the erection of new headquarters for the Co-operative Union Limited in Manchester, for the purpose of perpetuating the life and works of G. J. Holyoake and his services to the Co-operative movement with a building bearing his name, in which facilities may be found for carrying on all kinds of work for the spread of Co-operative ideals. £20,000 is required, and other Societies have similarly contributed their quota.

Our annual subscription to the funds of the Co-operative Union Limited was also increased by the Committee to £13 10s.

On Whit Saturday over 400 members and friends contributed largely towards a successful excursion arranged by the Society to Cleethorpes. A very enjoyable day was spent, and the Grimsby Co-operative Society kindly provided a capital breakfast for our party. It was a long journey to Cleethorpes, but was fully compensated in the pleasure obtainable there, and we had the benefit of fair weather. Events of this nature produce very pleasant social intercourse, and it is regrettable that more do not take advantage of the opportunities provided.

Mill Street Premises.

It was decided by the Committee early in the year to alter the construction of our Mill Street premises to provide greater accommodation for facilitating the increasing business at that branch. The present butchery shop will be taken in with the grocery shop, and a new shop erected on the yard space of the Grocery Department in Elm Street for the Butchery. The work was given to Messrs. Wooller and Sons (Eccles), who have erected two other splendid shops for us, one of which was a similar undertaking. They are now in course of alteration, and the ultimate result will be surprising, and greatly compensate for previous inconvenience. We, therefore, hope to receive our members' forbearance a little longer.

A portable building has been placed upon the vacant land in Vincent Street to serve the purpose of a butcher's shop until such time that a permanent structure is erected. This should provide a convenience for our Vincent Street friends, and at the same time keep their trade within the movement.

Other important decisions arrived at by the Committee now waiting to be put into operation are :—The supply of pure farm milk to our members ; a system of goods delivery to members in outside districts ; and the alteration of the Society's rules to allow our stocks to be taken, and a balance sheet published, half yearly instead of quarterly as at present. The latter, in the words of one of our *confrères*, will be " a maximum amount of advantage with a minimum amount of risk."

RECAPITULATION.

Members will no doubt have observed during the perusal of the foregoing pages that the Society was considerably handi-capped for many years in not having been able to secure property of its own for want of capital, and consequently had to rent property on heavy charges. When able to secure property, the only choice was old property on account of price, which would be subject to reconstruction in after years. It was, therefore, essential that the Committee should make due provision in the depreciation account for the purpose of rebuilding at as early a date as possible. This forethought has proved a wise policy, for, at the time of writing, Parker Street old property is cleared off the books and now rebuilt, and the Beswick shops are also cleared for future attention.

Some people are apt to think that by depreciation and various reserve funds created out of disposable balances Committees do a great deal too much for posterity, but it is only by these means that a Society can be placed in a good, sound financial position, and made secure for the years to come. The members should, therefore, give every indulgence to the Committee in the disposal of quarterly balances, and not desire all paid away in dividends. The Society is now, by its previous preparation, able to build new premises, instead of having to rent all premises—a source of continual and heavy expense ; has splendid reserves for various contingencies, which are being added to quarter by quarter ; and possesses splendid assets in the buildings and fixtures account.

A perusal of the Society's quarterly balance sheet should convince the most sceptical of persons that the Beswick Co-operative Society is in a sound financial position ; one of the most up-to-date ; and is one that welcomes all classes of people as its members, poor as well as rich, without any class distinction, all on one basis, receiving one benefit.

In conclusion, it is hoped that what has been recorded may prove to be interesting and instructive. The main object has been to state the true position and career of the Society without fear or favour, and I trust that that object has been attained.

An appendix follows of figures showing the progress of the Society, added instead of placing amongst the records, which should prove an easy means of reference to our position, as it were, in a nutshell.

In taking leave I trust the essence may lead to a better knowledge of our Society, and that our members may be the means of making it more widely known, so that others who have not yet joined the Society may be induced to jo'n, and so reap the same benefits that 7,000 receive. The entrance fee, I would remind you, is only 6d., and therefore should not debar the poorest of persons. Our hospitality is open to all.

May success continue to follow the stride of the Beswick Co-operative Society.

A. E. W.

Appendix.

PROVISIONAL COMMITTEE, 1892.

President : Mr. ARTHUR CUSS.

Mr. J. W. CALLISON.	Mr. J. PLATT.
„ DRINKWATER.	„ J. PICKVANCE.
„ HOLROYDE.	„ W. HILTON THOMPSON.
„ J. HURST.	„ JOHN BOYS, Sec. *pro. tem.*

Mr. JOHN T. DOBSON, *Manager.*

COMMITTEE.

Presidents : Mr. A. CUSS, 1892–1897.   Mr. G. E. STOTT, 1897–1907 (by death).
Mr. W. BROOKS, 1907*.

Mr. J. ASHWORTH, 1892 (9 months)	Mr. R. TAYLOR, 1894–1896
„ J. BERRY, 1892 (3 months)	„ G. E. STOTT, 1894–1897
„ E. CONNELL, 1892 (6 months)	(President)
„ J. HURST, 1892 (6 months)	„ W. BROOKS, 1895–1907
„ J. PLATT, 1892 (9 months)	(President)
„ G. POOLE, 1892–1896	„ A. SCHOFIELD, 1896–1898,
„ S. B. RAMSBOTTOM, 1892	1898–1900, 1905*
(3 months)	„ J. ANDREWS, 1896 (6 months)
„ J. RUDDOCK, 1892 (6 months)	„ T. CHADWICK, 1896*
„ J. NUTTALL, 1893 (9 months)	„ J. W. COLES, 1896*
1894*	„ M. ROBERTS, 1897 (6 months)
„ J. T. BLEASE, 1893–1896,	„ P. RYDER, 1898–1903,
1896–1898	1904–1905
„ J. HALL, 1893–1896	„ R. S. CLARK, 1898–1900
„ W. TAPLIN, 1893–1897, 1903*	„ E. TAYLOR, 1898*
„ J. KNOWLES, 1893 (3 months)	„ G. KILBOURNE, 1900*
„ FROST, 1893–1894	„ W. WALKER, 1900*
„ A. BORSEY, 1893–1894,	„ T. PHILLIPS, 1903*
1897–1904	„ W. ALCOCK, 1907*
„ NIGHTINGALE, 1893–1895	

ELECTED OFFICERS, &c.

Secretary :	*Manager :*
Mr. J. ASHHURST, 1892–1896	Mr. J. T. DOBSON, 1892–1896
„ A. E. WORSWICK, 1896*	„ W. RODDIS, 1896*

Auditors :	*Editor :*
Mr. J. FLETCHER, 1892–1895	Mr. A. CUSS, 1896–1898
„ W. H. AXON, 1892–1897	„ W. KAYTON, 1898–1899
„ J. H. CHADWICK, 1895*	„ R. S. CLARK, 1899–1900
„ J. ASHHURST, 1897–1904–1906*	„ J. ROWBOTTOM, 1900–1902
„ R. S. CLARK, 1904–1906	„ S. Tyldesley, 1902*

*Present Officials.

STATISTICS—Quarterly since Establishment, June, 1892.

Quarter.	Sales.			Dividend.			Rate per £.		Interest.			Share Capital.			Members.
	£	s.	d.	£	s.	d.	s.	d.	£	s.	d.	£	2.	d.	
1892–1st… …………	794	19	6½	14	0	0	1	0	3	4	8	274	7	6	76
2nd (14 wks.)	9:6	2	7	25	17	4	1	4	3	18	4	395	8	11	95
3rd …………	875	17	1	38	18	4	1	8	4	18	5	425	14	0	121
1893–4th …………	996	5	6	45	8	4	1	8	5	1	9	456	12	10	147
5th …………	1149	4	2	61	15	8	1	10	5	7	6	484	3	0	175
6th …………	1218	3	8	81	8	0	2	0	5	15	4	541	16	9	205
7th …………	1597	2	4	121	6	0	2	0	6	5	0	880	15	9	294
1894–8th …………	1750	15	0	143	14	0	2	0	6	11	2	629	12	2	357
9th …………	1870	14	0	158	18	0	2	0	6	17	7	648	4	3	394
10th …………	1990	1	2	188	14	4	2	2	7	5	3	707	17	10	427
11th …………	2314	6	8	219	16	2	2	2	7	19	7	853	2	0	463
1895–12th …………	2267	16	2	230	4	2	2	2	9	11	9	971	12	3	513
13th ………	2435	6	11	241	18	2	2	2	10	15	11	1072	19	1	633
14th (14 wks.)	3782	17	11	379	16	4	2	2	13	4	7	1397	3	6	735
15th (15 „)	3972	19	7	492	5	0	2	6	16	10	11	1560	4	4	787
1896–16th …………	3333	5	3	428	10	0	2	6	12	5	5	1173	18	6	904
17th …………	4185	13	0	570	5	4	2	8	13	6	6	1346	3	4	1003
18th …………	5046	7	1	769	9	4	2	8	15	15	2	1635	1	8	1148
19th (12 wks.)	6193	4	6	837	3	2	2	8	19	6	8	1975	4	1	1286
1897–20th …………	6118	0	3½	788	17	4	2	8	20	8	10	2090	3	3	1336
21st …………	6018	2	7½	766	1	4	2	8	22	0	3	2473	6	10	1421
22nd…………	7054	1	3½	893	14	8	2	8	27	15	0	2966	8	2	1582
23rd…………	7969	18	2½	1034	10	8	2	8	32	3	6	3303	19	8	1691
1898–24th …………	8188	3	6½	11 7	5	5	2	8	36	7	9	4123	1	2	1770
25th …………	8015	13	2½	1016	6	5	2	9	45	4	9	4666	12	4	1914
							6d. Butch'ry								
26th …………	9745	9	5	1234	13	5	2	9	50	15	0	5178	8	6	2038
							1/1 Butch'ry								
27th …………	10397	7	6½	1377	0	1	2	9	57	12	6	6037	12	9	2138
							2/6 Butch'ry								
1899–28th …………	10355	17	0	1428	4	9	2	10	64	18	8	6446	19	3	2220
29th …………	10752	2	4	148)	7	9	2	10	67	13	5	6766	4	8	2347
30th …………	12442	1	1½	1716	18	4	2	10	74	13	2	7557	7	6	2505
31st …………	13625	0	6½	1878	1	9	2	10	82	1	3	8295	6	3	2673
1900–32nd…………	14110	17	6	1938	13	0	2	10	89	16	0	8904	16	9	2928
33rd…………	14907	8	3½	2031	19	9	2	10	98	7	1	9841	16	10	3155
34th …………	15818	10	5½	2182	3	1	2	10	109	1	7	10813	3	8	3265
35th …………	16528	3	10½	2300	2	1	2	10	117	13	5	11506	14	8	3377
1901–36th …………	15869	9	1½	2089	13	2	2	9	122	6	11	11628	11	10	3339
37th …………	14988	9	1	1976	18	8	2	9	117	2	3	11359	11	4	3365
38th ………	16402	15	2½	2199	1	11	2	9	121	16	1	11873	5	2	3397
39th (12 wks.)	18335	3	8	2439	6	4	2	9	132	10	0	13125	19	10	3582
1902–40th (14 „)	21185	15	10	2744	5	7	2	8	145	7	11	13842	9	11	3629
41st …………	19853	3	3½	2662	19	6	2	9	158	2	3	14941	6	4	3829
42nd…………	22199	1	6	2949	0	0	2	9	167	7	7	15819	12	8	3923
43rd…………	23899	17	4	3179	14	1	2	9	183	17	9	17492	11	8	4128
1903–44th …………	23572	10	3½	3161	13	8	2	9	196	13	2	18624	11	10	4254
45th …………	23246	6	0	3095	6	2	2	9	207	13	8	19902	1	5	4430
46th …………	24955	15	0	3283	1	11	2	9	227	1	8	21277	13	8	4468
47th …………	25459	16	11	3431	14	5	2	9	249	5	1	23532	2	7	4741
1904–48th …………	26231	9	4	3485	11	10	2	9	260	13	4	23795	8	4	5043
49th ………	27524	8	11	3668	19	5	2	9	265	4	10	25060	13	2	5527
50th (14 wks.)	34043	0	2	4575	14	11	2	9	286	8	4	26913	8	8	5786
51st …………	32779	11	8	4412	12	7	2	9	310	6	11	29419	13	7	5993
1905–52nd…………	30149	0	0	4006	19	6	2	9	329	3	11	30377	5	0	5926
53rd …………	28499	8	9½	3809	6	2	2	9	335	10	1	32001	5	7	5987
54th …………	33303	12	0	4468	15	11	2	9	360	17	2	33601	4	0	6121
55th …………	35312	8	2½	4731	3	5	2	9	386	5	5	36528	18	5	6284
1906–56th …………	34227	0	4	4577	17	8	2	9	403	14	4	37298	6	4	6325
57th …………	32955	7	3	4416	0	11	2	9	411	5	1	38632	14	7	6468
58th …………	37345	7	0	5002	13	5	2	9	447	5	6	41463	3	1	6510
59th (12 wks.)	35021	7	1	4698	6	6	2	9	475	19	8	44799	2	4	6629
1907–60th (14 „)	41256	2	4	5467	18	7	2	9	494	14	11	45331	15	5	6677

THE FOREGOING COMPUTED IN YEARS SHOWS
THE ABNORMAL PROGRESS OF THE SOCIETY DURING THE
PAST FIFTEEN YEARS ENDED JULY, 1907.

Year.	Sales.			Dividend.			Interest.			Share Capital.			Membership.
	£	s.	d.	£	s.	d.	£	s.	d.	£	s.	d.	
*1893 ..	3583	4	8½	124	4	0	17	3	2	456	12	10	147
1894 ..	5715	5	2	408	3	8	23	19	0	629	12	2	357
1895 ..	8442	18	0	797	12	8	31	14	2	971	12	3	513
†1896 ..	13524	9	8	1542	9	6	52	16	10	1173	18	6	904
‡1897 ..	21543	4	10½	2965	15	2	68	17	2	2090	3	3	1336
1898 ..	29230	5	8	3801	12	1	118	6	6	4123	1	2	1770
1899 ..	38514	7	2	5056	4	8	218	10	11	6446	19	3	2220
1900 ..	50930	1	6	7014	0	10	314	3	10	8904	16	9	2938
1901 ..	63123	11	9	8603	18	1	447	9	0	11628	11	10	3339
1902 ..	70912	3	10	9359	12	6	516	16	3	13842	9	11	3629
1903 ..	89524	12	5	11953	7	3	706	0	9	18624	11	10	4254
1904 ..	99893	7	3	13295	14	4	944	13	9	23795	8	4	5043
*1905 ..	124496	0	9	16664	6	5	1191	4	0	30377	5	0	5926
1906 ..	131342	9	4	17587	3	2	1486	7	0	37298	6	4	6325
1907 ..	146578	3	8	19584	19	5	1829	5	2	45331	15	5	6677
TOTAL £	897354	5	9	118759	3	9	7967	7	6	45331	15	5	6677
Increase 1907 over first year	142994	18	11½	19460	15	5	1812	2	0	44875	2	7	6530

* 53 weeks.   † 55 weeks.   ‡ 51 weeks.

DISPOSAL OF THE BALANCES

IN ADDITION TO DIVIDENDS, INTEREST, AND BONUS TO EMPLOYEES DURING THE FIFTEEN YEARS.

SUBSCRIPTIONS :—	£	s.	d.	£	s.	d.
Ancoats Hospital	117	12	0			
Bradford Nurses' Home	66	3	0			
Children's Hospital	9	9	0			
R.S.P C.A.	10	10	0			
N.S.P.C.C.	9	9	0			
Old Folks' Party (local)	6	6	0			
				219	9	0
DONATIONS :—						
Various Objects	75	14	0			
Beswick Women's Guild	15	0	0			
				90	14	0
FUNDS :—						
Reserve	1544	0	0			
Dividend Equalisation	1013	0	0			
Educational Purposes	370	0	0			
Special Repairs	341	0	0			
Plate Glass Insurance	75	0	0			
Employés' Compensation Insurance	290	0	0			
				3633	0	0
Extra Depreciation on Buildings, Fixtures, and Rolling Stock				2740	18	5
Shares Depreciated				203	0	0
				£6887	1	5

FROM THE CO-OPERATIVE WHOLESALE SOCIETY WE HAVE RECEIVED IN

	£	s.	d.	£	s.	d.
Interest on Shares	1220	0	8			
,, Loans	218	5	11			
				1438	6	7
Dividends				8673	16	11
				£10112	3	6

First Dividend, 10s. 5d. Last Dividend, £766. 10s. 8d.

CPSIA information can be obtained
at www.ICGtesting.com
Printed in the USA
BVHW041515181219
567060BV00021B/1370/P